A GUIDE
TO MARXISM

A GUIDE
TO MARXISM

Joseph Martin

St. Martin's Press
New York

ISBN 0-312-35297-2

Library of Congress Cataloging In Publication Data

Martin, Joseph, 1920-
  A guide to Marxism.

  Bibliography: p.
  Includes index.
  1. Communism — History.   2. Socialism — History.
3. Marx, Karl, 1818-1883.   I. Title.
HX36.M34 1980   335.4   79-20376
ISBN 0-312-35297-2

Contents

Acknowledgements

I wish to express my deeply felt gratitude to all those who have given me valuable advice and friendly encouragement while I was working on this book. My particular thanks go to Dr Edward N. Allen, of the University of Queensland, and to my friend Arthur Weetman. Both have sacrificed considerable time in reading and criticizing successive drafts of the manuscript. My gratitude also goes to my wife without whose support and infinite patience this book may not have reached the publication stage.

Introduction

In 1848 Karl Marx, in collaboration with his associate Friedrich Engels, published the *Communist Manifesto*. It is one of the outstanding documents of all time. Its historical significance is comparable to that of the American Declaration of Independence of 1776 and the French Declaration of the Rights of Man of 1789. From the vision laid down in the *Manifesto* grew a new order that, though inconsistent with many of their ideas, today rules one-third of the world.

Marx grew up in Prussia, an oppressive state that was going through the beginning of a period of turbulent transition from the agrarian to the industrial age. As farms were being consolidated into larger units and factory-type production was increasing, small farmers and other small producers were being ruined and forced into unspeakable living conditions around factories, while inside the factories workers suffered severe hardship. The hours worked each day were growing longer, wages were falling, and women and children were being employed in increasing numbers. Children as young as eight years old were made to work as much as fourteen hours a day in mills and mines.

Marx damned this system in which "all that is holy is being profaned" and his imaginative genius led him to produce a theory that showed that man would be liberated from these inhuman conditions of life. Like every other intellectual, he extracted from the existing ideas what he needed and rejected the rest. By drawing on the German idealistic philosophy, on the French socialist schools of thought, and on the classical school of British political economy, he produced a new interpretation of man, society, and history that was to introduce totally new expectations into human affairs.

His work also greatly enriched all social sciences. He has grasped and presented, as nobody before him did, the importance of technological progress and the cultural superstructure created to serve its needs. Economics, according to Marx, is the prime determinant of man's ideas and values, his social relations, his institutions and the kind of government under which he lives, as well as his religious concepts and artistic expressions. His theory of the relationship between the nature of man, freedom, and alienation is receiving increasing attention in Western societies — more particularly among the young academics. Marx, who had drawn so heavily on the European culture, in turn became an integral part of it. Often, without our being conscious of the fact, the way we think and the way we look at the world have been moulded by Marx's ideas. Many things are held to be true because Marx said so.

"Marxists" have interpreted his theory in a manner that can only be described as creative. In accordance with their recognition of the current needs and conditions in their country, by way of "logical deduction", they have selected some concepts while ignoring others. In other words, in its practical application, Marxism has suffered the fate of other ideologies: it has become a storehouse from which various strategies and diverse tactics can be supported.

But, although the tenets of modern communism are not identical with the classical Marxian conception, the latter still has a great deal of vitality left in it. The Communists never forget Marx's theoretical principles. They are recognized as the basic philosophy from which today's Communist dogma has developed. In the Communist countries Marx's theory represents a science and the source of all truth. Being their conventional wisdom and the basis of morality, it provides justification for their institutions and practices — and for the leaders of the Communist Party to hold power.

Outside the Communist world, Marxism provides a guideline for political parties, trade unions, and other movements. And, because Marx had articulated the hopes and fears of the industrial age, it is intellectually an exciting force: perhaps not so much for the answers it gives (which tend to be ambiguous and inadequate) as for the questions it poses. Social critics and students all over the world study Marxist history, political science, sociology, and economics. To many young people Marxism represents a humanitarian philosophy oriented towards the future. Marx has become their accepted philosopher; his theory provides them with a different model in which to believe.

In view of the relevance of Marxism at the present time, the general public ought to familiarize itself with Marx's most important ideas. Millions who have never read a single line of what he had written, or who have read some of it but did not understand his long-winded and difficult prose, either blindly worship him or blindly hate him.

This book is designed not to propagandize but to provide, in a summary and simplified way, and as fairly as possible, an outline of the ideas basic to the Marxian doctrine and to discuss briefly the way in which it came to be applied. For the sake of brevity and logical continuity, some precision had to be sacrificed. Also, references to sources are omitted because they are of interest only in specialized studies and tend to frighten the general reader. There is no room for strict academic pendantry in the compilation of an easily digestible account of such a complex subject.

A knowledge of Marxism, apart from being a valuable addition to any person's intellectual store, has practical applications: it puts him in a better position to analyze social and political developments in Marxian terms. Ignorance of the essentials of Marxism, and thus of the Communist frame of reference, might impair our ability to cope with the world's problems successfully. Because we must coexist with the Communist world, and with those in our midst who sympathize with part or the whole of Marx's ideas, we should know more about the classical conception and how it is used, and misused, as an ideology for political purposes. Though Marx is out of date, one cannot afford to forget him.

1

Marx the Man

Karl Heinrich Marx was born in Prussia in 1818. He was the son of a Jewish lawyer and the grandson of a rabbi. The time of his birth coincided with the period when the defeat of Napoleon was complete and his egalitarian laws were being rescinded all over Europe. In Prussia one of the new edicts demanded that, once again, those holding official positions must be Christians. Because of it, Marx's father, who was in government employ, decided to convert himself and later the whole family to Protestantism. Young Karl was baptized when he was six years old.

As it was customary in those days to follow in one's father's footsteps, Marx began his university career by studying law. Later he combined law with philosophy. Towards the end of his studies his interests were confined to philosophy. While at the university — the only place in Prussia where the authorities still tolerated a small measure of freedom of speech — Marx demonstrated very strong commitment to the prevailing philosophical interest in the nature of freedom and self-determination and joined the Young Hegelians (whose ideas are discussed in the next chapter).

After graduation, Marx applied for a university position but was rejected because his views were regarded as too nonconformist. Instead he turned to journalism. He joined the staff of a liberal newspaper, the *Rheinische Zeitung*, and soon after became its editor-in-chief. While working on the paper he broke away from the vague sentimental longing for liberty of his student days and shifted his attention to politics and material realities. The paper came out strongly against certain laws that were causing economic distress to farmers. It also published strong anti-Russian articles. Censorship became stricter and stricter. In January 1843 the *Rheinische Zeitung* was ordered to close by 31 March on the ground that it had maliciously slandered state authorities and offended foreign powers. Marx, in an effort to save the paper, resigned and accepted full blame, but to no avail.

Intending to continue his radical journalism, Marx decided to leave for Paris, as France had a semi-free press. Before he left he married Jenny von Westphalen, to whom he had been engaged for seven years. Jenny, who was four years older than Marx, was the daughter of an eminent government official — a state councillor — and on her mother's side was a descendant of a Scottish nobleman. She had an aristocratic upbringing and was described by those who knew her as good looking, intelligent, cultured, and charming.

In Paris, in association with other German radicals, Marx set out to publish Franco-German annals — *Deutsch-Franzosische Jahrbucher* — a political review designed to combine German philosophy with French radical politics. But they could not attract a single French contributor; the French radicals were more interested in immediate practical politics than in idealistic philosophy that would convert only the highly educated. Moreover, few were prepared to accept the atheistic views of its German contributors. Only one bilingual issue was published. The German edition was banned in Germany, and the French one drew little comment in the French newspapers.

Nevertheless, Marx was to find in Paris not only a haven but also an inspiration. The revolutions of 1789 and 1830 had made France the undisputed centre of socialist thought and action. It is therefore not surprising that it was in Paris that his philosophical preoccupation with freedom and self-determination of his student days developed into an interest in the social conditions under which a free society would come about.

It was also in Paris that Marx began his all-important life-long association with Friedrich Engels. Engels, though the son of a rich German manufacturer, was an active radical. Unlike

Marx, Engels had lived from his earliest childhood among factories and slums. He grew up surrounded by the horrors of early capitalism: the poverty and distress of half-starved men, women, and children working at the loom for up to sixteen hours a day. As a young man he had been sent by his father to work in the family cotton-spinning factory in Manchester, the centre of the English cotton industry — the most modern industry in the most industrialized country in the world at the time. His *Conditions of the Working Class in England*, written in the winter 1844/45, gave Marx an insight into the dehumanizing social conditions of the workers under the new industrial system. Proclaiming that material forces were dominating men and their lives, instead of the other way round, Marx began to study economics. He ceased to regard the educated middle class as the agents for change; victory had to be achieved in the world of reality and not in the intellectual sphere. Having observed the spirit of revolt of the Parisian workers, he had come to the conclusion that the illiterate poor were not — as he had previously believed — merely a living example of the irrationality of the existing state, but that they were the vehicle of history. Since they were deprived of all property and therefore subject to exploitation, the poor would make the abolition of any system built on private property their guiding principle. And, by emancipating themselves, they would liberate mankind, because no type of enslavement could be terminated unless all enslavement were destroyed.

Paris, at the time regarded by all radicals as "the cradle of the new Europe", was the Mecca of its revolutionaries. Thus Marx became involved in the ferment that was to bring on the revolutions of 1848. To suppress his activities, the Prussian government exerted pressure on the French authorities to expel him. In 1845 he was ordered to leave France. Marx went to Brussels, where he obtained permission to stay only after he signed a promise to abstain from political activity. When the Prussian police demanded his extradition from the Belgians, Marx renounced his Prussian citizenship.

Despite his undertaking to abstain from political activity, Marx, who was soon joined in Brussels by Engels, was politically active in the three years he spent there. Together with

Engels, he established a Communist Correspondence Committee with the aim of putting German socialists in touch with English and French socialists. They expected to "obtain an exchange of ideas and impartial criticism" and, by bringing differences of opinion to light, eventually to give a more definite form to communism and to rid it of the limitations imposed by nationalism. This project had only limited success; very few correspondence committees were established. But it had one important result: it created a close link between Marx and Engels and London, where the largest and best-organized colony of German workers lived. These German expatriates believed that the cultivation of intellectual faculties would have to precede any physical uprising designed to lead man to liberty. As a result they concentrated their activity mainly on workers' education.

But there were also a number of more radical organizations. In the mid-1830s, when conspiratorial secret societies were common all over Europe, a small group of German artisans living in Paris had founded a semi-secret Communist association which they called the League of the Just. Its motto was "All men are brothers." After 1839 most of its members had moved to London. Marx and Engels recognized that through the League of the Just they could enter working-class politics. After managing to remove the artisans' mistrust of the "intellectual", they were invited to join. They persuaded its members to give the League an international rather than a German character, to change its name to Communist League and — arguing that communism must be based on scientific understanding and not just on emotional egalitarian principles — to draft a firmer theoretical definition of their aims. New statutes were adopted that proclaimed the establishment of a new social order without classes and without property as the League's paramount aim. In 1847 Marx and Engels were given the task of preparing a manifesto that would publicize their new doctrine.

At the time, there were three strains of socialism. The main body of Socialist organizations desired merely the elimination of social abuses within the existing order by appealing to those in power on the basis of reason and justice. The second com-

prised the declining number of "utopians" who tried to practise Socialist principles in isolated communities.* And third,
there were a handful of "Communists" who denounced the
power that the monopoly of property gave some men over
other men and strongly believed in the imminence of a workers' revolution that would destroy this unjust social order; but
they lacked any definite policy. Marx and Engels denounced
the Socialists as a lower-middle class conservative movement
who looked to the "educated classes" for support, and they
dismissed the utopians on the ground that their approach was
based on little else but wishful thinking. They declared that the
emancipation of the working class must be the act of the working class itself and in this spirit set out to give the Communists
a programme. The *Communist Manifesto* outlined the historical
process by which society was being transformed so that the
working class could consciously participate in it. It proclaimed
the inevitable dissolution of private property and its passing into a higher form of common ownership.

When writing the *Manifesto*, Marx and Engels knew that in
parts of Europe revolution was brewing. There had been isolated rebellions against working conditions, and they concluded that in the industrial countries the workers were ready
for revolt. In their revolutionary zeal, they did not confine the
Manifesto to giving a theoretical Communist programme but
included a passionate call for revolutionary action. They called
upon the workers to overthrow the existing social order; the
working class could liberate itself from exploitation and oppression "only by the forcible overthrow of all existing social
conditions. Let the ruling classes tremble at the Communist
revolution. The workers have nothing to lose but their chains.
They have a world to gain." The *Manifesto* concluded with the
call "Workers of all countries, unite!"

---

* Utopian ideals had inspired social philosophers and visionaries for a long
time. They originated in Plato's *Republic* and his *Laws*. Utopians envisaged a
perfect state in which justice, freedom, equality, and fraternity prevail, and
all is ordered for the welfare of its citizens. At times, idealists had withdrawn
into utopian communities and tried to practise these principles. However,
none of these communities were successful, and they only proved that, at
least where there is a scarcity, it is beyond the grasp of human nature to be
voluntarily indifferent to status and material goods.

The *Communist Manifesto* was published in London by a German printer in February 1848 — the year of revolutions in France, Germany, Austria, and Hungary. In the excitement of these events, its publication went virtually unnoticed.

The industrial crisis of 1847, which was the prelude to the revolutionary period of 1848, was particularly severe in Belgium. There was widespread political unrest in which the foreign political exiles living in Belgium played an active part. The government decided to expel them, and on 3 March 1848 Marx was given twenty-four hours to leave the country. He went first to Paris, where the revolution had the upper hand at the time; then he and other members of the Communist League returned to Germany to take part in the revolutionary movement. They dispersed to various towns with the intention of establishing a national network. Most went to where they had lived before going into exile. Marx settled in Cologne, the biggest city in the most industrialized part of Germany, where he became the driving force behind the *Neue Rheinische Zeitung*.

Following the principles laid down by the *Communist Manifesto*, the *Neue Rheinische Zeitung* called upon the workers to take an active part in the revolution. At first it proclaimed that the task of the workers was to support the radical wing of the middle class to achieve its own emancipation — but with concessions to workers and peasants. There could be no talk of the immediate realization of socialism. The "forces of reaction" — defined as absolute monarchism and feudal domination — had to be destroyed first, because they restricted the development of modern industry which would create the material and political preconditions for the workers' own revolution and the foundation of a society in which everybody would become free. Once the middle class acceded to power, the working class would begin its role of being the opposition. But when the "middle class did not make its own revolution", the *Neue Rheinische Zeitung* changed its policy. It declared that the working class had to rely on its own forces and do it for them.

The events of 1848 developed quite differently from what Marx and Engels had advocated. In Germany the revolts were very localized, and only in Berlin was there serious violence. The revolutions were fought by nationalists and liberals — and their causes were independence, democracy, and land reform. The industrial workers — which, in any case, because of the still basically agrarian world of the time, represented only a small proportion of the population — played a negligible role. Notwithstanding their relative unimportance, after the revolts were crushed all workers' movements were ruthlessly hunted down. Marx, despite the wide popularity the *Neue Rheinische Zeitung* enjoyed, had been harassed by the authorities and repeatedly taken to court. In a major case, when he was charged with high treason for having urged people to refuse to pay taxes, Marx made such an eloquent speech at his trial that the jury acquitted him and the foreman of the jury thanked him on behalf of his colleagues for his "extremely informative speech". Nevertheless, Marx, who had renounced his citizenship a few years earlier, was expelled from Germany for being an "alien" disturber of peace and order. The last issue of the *Neue Rheinische Zeitung* appeared two days later — printed in red.

Marx arrived in Paris penniless. The *Neue Rheinische Zeitung* had swallowed up all of his and his wife's money. The French authorities gave him the choice of residing in the provinces or leaving France. He decided to leave and, in August 1849, still a young man of only thirty-one, settled in London, the "mother of exiles". Here he was to spend the remaining thirty-four years of his life, living with his wife and three children (three other children had died young) in comparative isolation and suffering much hardship. They lived in ugly insanitary tenements, and there were times when they were reduced to the point of starvation and had to pawn the children's shoes and clothing. Marx, who in 1841 had been declared unfit for military service "owing to the sensitivity of his lungs", is said to have been in pain much of the time. He suffered from an enlarged liver, haemorrhoids, and recurrent boils and eye infections.

When Marx first arrived in London, he predicted that England would go through an economic crisis in the autumn of 1850 and was politically active expecting the outbreak of another revolution. But Marx did not believe that the impending revolution had any prospect of success; he had accepted the view that the struggle would take a long time. In an

Address to the Central Committee of the Communist League, issued to branches in March 1850, he declared that it was the task of the League to make the revolution — started by the petty middle-class in 1848 — permanent until in all the dominant countries of the world at least the decisive instruments of production were in the hands of the workers. When the crisis failed to appear, and Europe was on the threshold of a period of prosperity and peace instead, Marx withdrew from revolutionary activity. Except for the period when he took part in the running of the First International (which is discussed elsewhere) he spent his days in endless research, writing, and polemics with a number of his contemporaries. The reading room of the British Museum was his second home. It was mostly here that he wrote the massive material for the three volumes of *Capital*, in which he formulated his principles in a scientific and abstract manner. In its essentials it is an elaboration and refinement of what the *Communist Manifesto* had proclaimed. The first and most important volume was published in 1867 while Marx was still alive; the other two were completed from a large number of notes and manuscripts and published post-humously by Engels.

Engels devoted his life to Marx. To enable Marx to pursue his literary work, he entered the Manchester branch of his father's business in 1850, and supported Marx as best he could. Although Marx's personal income was small, it would have been enough had it been carefully managed; he contributed to a number of periodicals and to the *New York Daily Tribune* — the paper with the largest circulation in the world at the time. However, it was only in the mid-1860s that his financial burdens eased. Engels, on his father's death, became a partner in the business and was able to give Marx a regular allowance. Without Engels, the proud, uncompromising, and financially careless Marx probably would have perished in London.

In 1870, after twenty years of separation, Engels sold his share in the business and moved to London to work beside Marx. In a self-effacing way, he compressed Marx's abstract concepts and applied them to current affairs. Although Engels succeeded in popularizing Marx (and probably saved him from remaining an obscure academic thinker), he is now accused by many Marxist scholars of having oversimplified Marx's subtle and complex ideas and divorced them from their philosophical base. Engels is said to have overemphasized economic satisfaction, while to Marx material wealth was merely a prerequisite for a free society and human dignity. However valid this modern view is, the ideas of both men make up what is now accepted as "classical Marxism" — or "Marxism-Engelism". In any case, it would be extremely difficult to separate completely the ideas of Engels from those of Marx.

By 1875 Marx's health had begun to deteriorate and his work slowed down. He died in 1883 at the age of sixty-five and was buried in the Highgate Cemetery. His grave, on which a marble block with a cast-iron head was erected in 1956, is today a tourist attraction.

Marx undoubtedly considered himself to be what the Germans call a *Gelehrter* — meaning a person who has deep knowledge and who applies himself with passion to systematize the answer to any question he sets himself. He was ceaselessly collecting material and did not finish anything until he had read everything that had been written about the subject. Moreover, Marx is quoted as saying: "Science should not be an egoistic pleasure. Those fortunate enough to devote themselves to scientific work should be the first to apply their knowledge in the service of humanity." And indeed, with courage, unshakeable conviction, and singleness of purpose, Marx dedicated himself to providing what he believed would give a scientific base to socialism, which he saw as the movement directed towards bringing about a new and better system of human relations. He mapped the road he thought would lead man out of the misery, exploitation, and alienation created by a society built on private property and division of labour. The new world to which this road led was one in which man — liberated from his material and spiritual shackles — would become a free, self-fulfilling human being engaged in harmonious labour with everyone else.

The purpose of the next chapter is to give an outline of Marx's conception.

2

Marxism: The Classical Conception

Karl Marx studied at the University of Berlin, where the philosopher Georg Wilhelm Friedrich Hegel had been teaching shortly before Marx became a student there. At the time, philosophy played a large part in university education; and philosophy in general — and Hegel in particular — had a profound influence on intellectual thinking all over Germany. There were many so-called Hegelian societies. Those referred to as the Hegelian Right represented the conservative strains of his thinking; while the Hegelian Left, or the Young Hegelians, attracted nonconformist younger intellectuals, including Marx.

To understand the intellectual roots of Marx's doctrine one must know something about the philosophical thoughts that influenced the Young Hegelians. It is beyond the scope of a short book such as this to attempt to explain the complexities of German philosophy as a whole. Nonetheless, in the next few paragraphs some of the concepts that were to provide Marx with the ground ideas of his work are outlined.

In their essence, the ideals of the Young Hegelians went back to the eighteenth century, to the Age of Enlightenment. In this period of great intellectual activity, a rationalist and liberal trend of thought among an idealistic élite was seeking self-emancipation from prejudice and conventions. They attributed human misery not only to unfortunate material conditions but also to the ignorance generated by the distortion of truth by both civil and religious authorities. The leaders of this movement believed that human nature is essentially rational and responsible, and that truly rational and responsible people co-operate with one another naturally and spontaneously. There-fore the divisions and conflict one finds in society have to be explained externally; values and attitudes imposed from out-side make people behave in a way that goes against their natu-ral instincts. They had limitless faith in the power of human reason to explain and improve the world once men were al-lowed to become self-determining individuals. This idea that men in co-operation with one another could bring about social change was a radical departure from the generally accepted as-sumptions at the time that all changes should be attributed to an "act of God" or to a "great man", a heroic genius, who emerges when the historical moment is right.

Immanuel Kant, the leading figure of German philosophy at the time of the Enlightenment, wrote: "So act as to treat hu-manity whether in your own person or that of another in every case as an end in itself, never as a means." He fought dog-matic religion by stressing the value of human reason and the autonomy of the human conscience as a source of obligations. He urged his fellow men to have faith in themselves and in the freedom of their will. Marx enthusiastically endorsed the notion of each man's individuality and uniqueness; also the belief in his essential rationality and goodness, and, therefore, his perfectibility. In the theory he was to develop, Marx en-visaged man creating in due course an ideal society in which he would enjoy the kind of freedom that would permit him to become a universal and truly self-determined human being.

Returning to Hegel: very simply and briefly, his philosophy was based on the idea that it was the fundamental nature of man to be constantly developing himself and, in co-operation with other men, transforming the world about him. Two of his concepts are of particular relevance to Marx's theory. One deals with alienation and the other with a new philosophy of history. Alienation, or estrangement, is an idea that dates back to the Greek philosophers. Saint Paul also alluded to it. Hegel held that man feels alienated because in society there is a master and serf relationship. There is oppression: one man dominates the other. Because man must belong to one of the social classes he becomes alienated from his true self: he must act in accordance with what is believed to be in the interest of his class, and this often forces him to act against his conscience. And man is alienated not only from himself but also from society. Because of his membership of one of the classes, he cannot freely co-operate with all his fellow men. He is at odds with the society he himself has made, of which he is a member and, indeed, which could not exist without his participation. Put in another way, man — who by nature is a creative being — instead of being a subject developing himself in collaboration with his fellow men, is turned into an object alienated from himself and his fellows.

But Hegel was optimistic about the final outcome. He was confident that man, who is by nature a rational being, would liberate himself. Because he viewed the state as the highest level of social organization, representing society becoming rational, he regarded it as the agent for man's liberation. The "ideal state" would reconcile individual needs with universal needs and remove all barriers to human development. Hegel considered that the state he described was to some extent already present in Prussia at the time. Also religion, which according to Hegel fulfilled man's psychological needs to have an image of himself and to orientate himself in the world around him, had found its highest and final form in Protestant Christianity. These assumptions were fully endorsed by the Hegelian Right and led many Germans to conclude that they were the leaders of humanity.

Hegel's philosophy of history is that history is a continuous dynamic process from a lower to a higher status of life. He drew on the technique called "dialectics", which was used by Socrates and other Greek philosophers in their attempts to arrive at the truth. By means of questions and answers, they reduced contradictory ideas into an organized whole. Hegel evolved the following dialectic pattern. He said that the history of mankind is real only if it is viewed as the history of ideas. (This accords with Plato's belief that ideas alone are real and phenomena are only the reflection.) At any one stage one set of ideas guides events, and this set of ideas sooner or later is opposed — or "negated" — by another set with which it must be reconciled; otherwise civilization would perish. The reconciliation between the two sets of ideas brings into being a new set of ideas which guides events until it in turn is found defective, opposed and eventually replaced. Hegel called this the "negation of the negation". In due course, this new set of ideas is negated and the process begins all over again. Each time a new set of ideas is accepted — having retained elements of the previous one and at the same time gone beyond it — it is of a higher order than the one which it replaced. This constant conflict of ideas goes on until the perfect Universal Idea emerges to which there can be no contradiction because of its completeness.

An important Young Hegelian was Ludwig Feuerbach, who is renowned both as a "materialist" and as a "humanist". He is described as a materialist because he once wrote that "man is what he eats". But more important is Feuerbach the humanist philosopher, who asserted the pre-eminence of man, in the sense that life precedes consciousness and ideas. He stated that ideas are not independent entities external to man but are the creation of man and, therefore, they cannot dominate man's fate as Hegel believed.

But Feuerbach made use of the Hegelian notion of alienation in his study of religion. In his *Essence of Christianity* (1841), he maintained that God did not create man in his image; on the contrary, man created God in his image — or rather in the image of what he might be if he fully realized himself. Religion was the essence of man projected outside himself. This projection by man of the powers and qualities that belong to his own being into an imaginary entity alienates his ability to develop to his fullest potential.

Feuerbach's views were echoed by Marx, who wrote that "religion has no content of its own and lives not from heaven but from earth", and that man "has found only a reflection of himself in the fantastic reality of heaven where he sought the supernatural being". And the more man attributes to God the less he has left himself. While Marx praised Feuerbach's "real humanism", and declared that man should be the highest being for man, he criticized him for treating man as an isolated being. Marx stressed that the human essence can be found only in the unity of man with man and, therefore, the true human being is revealed only in society. Marx was to extend Feuerbach's humanistic image of the individual and his potentials into a concept of man in the mesh of human relations.

As can be seen from the outline given above, the Young Hegelians considered true morality to be independent of religion and to be based on the autonomy of man. Man should be free to determine his essential nature, his will, and his place in society. Since they were critics of religious dogmas, repressive laws, and censorship, the authorities treated them as radicals.

Throughout his life, Marx accepted with deep conviction as his prime goal the need for freedom to develop human needs and faculties. Again and again he wrote about the "free activity of man". But to Marx, freedom did not denote freedom to own and acquire property, freedom to better oneself materially, freedom of religion, and so on. On the contrary, it meant freedom from craving for possessions and from competitive acquisitiveness, from religious dogma, from state authority, and from all other facets of man's environment that take away, or "alienate", from him opportunities to develop his essential human nature.

The interrelation and interdependence between the nature of man, freedom, and alienation occupy a central position in Marx's theory. Marx attributed to man "natural powers", or capacities which he shares with other living creatures, and "species powers" — meaning a wide range of potentialities that set humans apart from, and gives them an advantage over, animals. Marx believed that man has an inner drive to cultivate his species powers and, being a social being, he can develop them only in community with his fellow men. Only where there is freedom and full co-operation with others can man activate his manifold latent physical and intellectual abilities, assert his true individuality, and develop into a whole human being.

In Marx's view, the prerequisite for what he understood to be freedom is a state of economic development in which man will have advanced beyond the stage of economic activity for the sake of survival. As long as man must live in the "realm of necessity" — because the existing productive assets and techniques are inadequate to supply his needs — there will be division of labour, greed, and competition separating man from man. And in a social order, established to avoid property, hunger, and wants in all its forms, man's position in society, his productive activity, and even the structure of his thoughts are determined for him. He is denied his right of becoming a fully realized individual. As a result, man is only a small part of what he should be.

The state, religion, and so on alienate man from some of his powers, but Marx's main emphasis was on the alienation man suffers while engaging in productive activity. As long as man lives in a world of necessity and he must devote so much of his time to production in order to survive, his productive work is the core of his life activity. To the great mass of people it is practically the whole of their life activity. Instead of nourishing their distinctive human powers, they are reduced to performing extremely one-sided repetitious labour. They are alienated from the chief opportunity through which they can express and develop themselves.

But, Marx asserted, productive assets were being accumulated and production techniques were being improved, and the time was approaching when man could cast off the limitations imposed on him by economic necessity. Once material needs were easily satisfied and he no longer sustained life in a manner that "fragments and disfigures" him, man would bring about a new order — a Communist society. In genuine co-operation with all his fellow men, he would create conditions in which he would enjoy freedom to apply himself to whatever activity he chose. In this "realm of freedom" there would be ever-widening opportunities to cultivate a "world of productive impulses and faculties". Individuals would realize their essential human nature and make the world part of themselves and themselves part of the world. For the first time in history, man would be a truly human — that is, unalienated — being.

Let us now look at Marx's total conception. For the convenience of those readers who have no ambition to become Marxian scholars and those who, wishing to pursue studies in particular aspects of this subject, are seeking some preliminary or background reading, it seems appropriate to present Marx's conception in three parts. The first deals with the notion of a historical evolutionary process, the second with the theory about the growth and decline of the capitalist system, and the third with the belief in the emergence of a "Communist" world.

The Historical Evolutionary Process

Marx made what he described as being a scientific inquiry to "find a new world from the critic of the old".* His goal was to discover the inner laws of motion leading to changes in the way societies were organized, and he produced a new approach to history. It is based on two broad concepts: the "material basis" of history — to which Engels referred as "materialistic determinism"; and the concept of an evolutionary process built on Hegel's dynamic law of history.

Materialistic determinism means that the way in which people organize their lives at any one time in their history is determined primarily — though by no means exclusively — by the prevailing modes of producing, distributing, and exchanging the commodities needed by the community. Marx argued that the reason for this materialistic dominance is that man must eat, drink, dress, and find shelter before he can concern himself with any other matter. Because of the necessity to support life, the "productive forces" — defined by Marx as the various forms of labour and the physical means used in production such as land, raw materials, instruments, tools, and the like — bring about a division of labour within the nation. This forces men into definite relationships with one another that he called "productive relations". Manufacturing labour is separated from commercial labour, and together they are sep-

* To Marx, "scientific" inquiry meant that it was based on the observation of the "real life-process" and divorced from morality and philosophy. Marx wrote that science "instead of descending from heaven to earth, ascends from earth to heaven". One must begin with the active man and by way of empirical observation — that is, observation free of any mystification and speculation — explain his actions and the development of his ideas and ideological reflexes.

arated from agricultural labour; at the same time, within these branches groups of individuals co-operate in distinct kinds of work. Marx wrote: "For as soon as labour is distributed, each man has a particular exclusive sphere of activity which is forced upon him and which he cannot escape. He is a hunter, a fisherman, a shepherd, or a critical critic, and must remain so if he does not want to lose his means of livelihood."

This division of labour in production leads not only to productive relations but also to corresponding property relations. They are two sides of the same coin. As a result, society is divided into classes. There are classes whose members own the means of production and those whose members own nothing but their labour power. In other words, an individual is either an employer or a worker. Because people must belong to the one class or the other "their position in life and their personal development are assigned to them by their class". Man, by virtue of his class position, has his choices severely limited. He has to accept a defined position, ideology, and interests. Because it "is not the consciousness of men that determines their being, but, on the contrary, their social being that determines their consciousness", the human being is lost in his class. Instead of asserting his true individuality, he is forced to wear a social character mask that distinguishes him from the members of other classes.

Marx said that the "modes of production", which comprise the abovementioned productive forces and relations, represent the "substructure" — that is, the economic foundation — of society. An immense "superstructure" comes into existence, its main function being to protect and safeguard this productive base. The superstructure embraces the complex political, legal, educational, spiritual, and artistic framework of society; the pattern of institutions, organizations, and chains of authority. In order to reconcile the members of society to the existing system, it moulds people's opinions, customs, and their moral and ethical values, also their expectations and behaviour pattern. (But, while the superstructure dominates society, it is always challenged. At first by the ideas, customs, and habits that were part of the superstructure in the preceding society and, as time passes, by forward-looking revolutionary ideas.)

It follows that, whenever new productive forces gain prominence, there is not only an emergence of new productive and property relations but also a transformation of the superstructure so that it assists material production instead of becoming fetters upon it. In the *Communist Manifesto*, Marx and Engels wrote: "Does it require deep intuition to comprehend that man's ideas, views and conceptions, in a word, man's consciousness, changes with every change in conditions of his material existence, in his social relations and in his social life? What else does the history of ideas prove than that intellectual production changes its character in proportion as the material production changes?"

Now to sum up Marx's concept of materialistic determinism. Until such time as man's physical needs are readily satisfied, the mode of production of material life will tend to be the dominant factor in establishing the necessity both of the order of things within a given historical epoch and of its transition into another order. It follows that the ultimate causes of social changes and political revolutions are to be sought in the economics of the period. Man is destined to change society whenever the material forces of production demand it. Social change being a historical necessity, man does not have a truly free choice in the matter. Circumstances compel him to develop a consciousness of his role and destiny which is to create an entirely new society whenever new forces of production come to predominate. Thus, although men make their history, the way and the conditions under which they make it and the direction it takes are not entirely under their control. Marx wrote that his task was to make man a conscious participator in the historical process of social revolution that is taking place before his eyes.

The second idea used by Marx to develop his theory of a historical evolutionary process was Hegel's dynamic law of history based on the dialectic pattern.

Marx went along with Hegel's idea that history was a series of evolutions resulting from the reconciliation of contradictions, but rejected some of his other assumptions. For instance, Marx wrote that to Hegel history had become the history of the abstract spirit of humanity — a spirit that is above and beyond the real man. Hegel developed the world out of what is logical, instead of developing the logical out of the world. Ideas do not create the real because reality is not of the mind but of matter. Independent thought cannot control events: ideas are merely the reflections of the material world translated into forms of thought. Therefore, the historical process is not determined by changing ideas but by man in response to changes in the production of material life itself, because production is "a fundamental condition of all history, which today, as thousands of years ago, must be accomplished every day and every hour merely in order to sustain human life". Marx took issue with Hegel on another point. He accused Hegel of regarding the task of philosophy as merely to provide an understanding of the present by explaining what happened in the past. "True philosophy", Marx argued, extends to the future. It is a weapon that changes the world — an instrument for political action.

This line of reasoning enable Marx to link his materialistic concept to Hegel's dialectic method. Declaring that the Hegelian dialectic was "standing on its head; it must be turned right side up", Marx replaced the contradictions between ideas with contradictions emerging within the mode of production and, more particularly, between social classes (a not unreasonable assumption at the time when society was rigidly divided into strata) and formulated a new theory of the historical evolutionary process that not only went back into history but also projected its future course.

According to Marx, the historical evolutionary process has its roots in the primitive tribal society in which man struggled to satisfy his basic needs of food by hunting, fishing, and cattle breeding. At this stage — called by Marx "communalism" or "primitive communism" — land belonged to nobody, and herds and flocks were the common property of the tribe.

But, once man's existing needs were met, he discovered new ones that demanded satisfaction. Agriculture developed, and with it came division of labour. As the means of subsistence available to man increased, so did population. When uncultivated land became scarce, land began to be claimed as communal as well as private property. The emergence of private property divided society into distinct social classes. One set of classes comprised those who had obtained control over land or who had accumulated other means of production; the other classes comprised those who had been unable to acquire property and therefore depended for their livelihood on those who had property. To put it into the dialectic framework, there came into being classes of "possessors" who were confronted by classes of "dispossessed". After the existing forces of production developed to their fullest extent and new ones appeared that more fully satisfied man's needs, there was a period of unrest because the relations of property — which corresponded to the requirements of the old forces of production — acted as fetters to the ones that were emerging. The dispossessed classes seized the opportunity to overthrow the possessors and to emancipate themselves. As the old order perished, a new one was created in which the relations of production and property better suited the needs of the new productive reality.

Among the forms of society in which productive and class relations were based upon the division of labour and private property, Marx recognized three "progressive epochs" that had unique and distinctive features and which represented a particular stage of development in the history of mankind. They were the ancient slave state, the feudal society, and the capitalist society. In the ancient slave state the freemen who owned the means of production were faced by slaves. When a new method of working land developed, changing society's economic foundation, the old ruling class became more and more parasitical on the new productive process. Thus a contradiction evolved between the new productive forces and the productive class relations established in the ancient slave state. The conflict between the classes created the situation in which this contradiction was overcome. The propertyless classes overthrew the old ruling classes, and this enabled the feudal lords, who were functionally indispensable to the new economic reality, to assume power. During the feudal epoch, a small-scale handicraft-type of production of trading goods was carried out within the guild system. In the new social class structure, the feudal lords and guild masters were confronted by the serfs and journeymen.

Towards the close of the Middle Ages, trade expanded rapidly and grew even faster after the discovery of America and the opening of Asia for trade. The "zeal displayed among the European nations in the race after the products of Asia and the treasures of America" gave commerce, navigation, and industry an impulse never known before. The feudal system of manufacture — in which production was monopolized by the restrictive guilds — could no longer supply the growing wants of the new markets. Larger-scale workshop production was developed by an emerging manufacturing middle class whose initial capital was the tools of their trade.

But markets kept on growing and demand rising. Even workshop manufacture no longer sufficed. Manpower and small tools came to be replaced by steam-power and machines, and workshops by giant industry. And "as industry, commerce, navigation, railways extended, in the same proportion the industrial capitalists developed, increased their capital, and pushed into the background every class handed down from the Middle Ages".

As the feudal productive arrangements were no longer compatible with the emerging productive forces, the feudal system tottered. The revolutionary element within the feudal society expanded quickly and the French Revolution of 1789 established the domination of the capitalist class. Thus from the ruins of the feudal system — dependent upon the hand mill — came the development of the capitalist system fostered by the introduction of steam power. And, instead of the country dominating the towns, the towns gradually assumed dominance over the country and, within the towns, commerce became subservient to industry.

Under the capitalist mode of production, capitalists, landowners, and wage labourers formed the great classes of society. Gradually the distinction between the landowner and the capitalist disappeared because the feudal character of landed property was lost. The landowner ceased to regard his land as property that passed from father to son. Land became purely another commodity — an object of speculation, and the landowner became just another capitalist. Thus, broadly speaking, the capitalists and the mass of wage labourers emerged as the decisive and historically determining classes.

While the capitalist owned the means of production Marx said he did not own the people he employed. Unlike the slave master and the feudal lord, he could not dispose of them as he liked. As the labourer had ceased to be a serf or the bondsman to another person, the capitalist epoch had ushered in an advance in freedom in the sense that the labourer could dispose of his labour power as his commodity. But this was all he could dispose of because he was robbed of whatever means of production he possessed and of all other guarantees of subsistence afforded to him by the earlier arrangements. He was thrust on the labour market and was an easy victim of its vagaries. Moreover — as is discussed in the next chapter — during the capitalist epoch the labourer's social interactions, which used to be personal, would become purely material. He would be ruthlessly exploited and suffer alienation to such a degree that it would have a debilitating effect on his physical and mental health.

Now to summarize Marx's philosophy of history. History is dominated by the need to produce the goods required for the satisfaction of man's wants. As time passes his desires expand and his creative ability enables him to develop new methods of production that will satisfy these needs. But this results in a change of the forces of production and brings them into conflict — what he called "objective contradiction" — with the existing class relations as they are fetters on the new productive reality. At a certain stage, the conflict between the decisive classes — that is, "the more or less veiled civil war raging within existing society" which Marx called "subjective contradiction" — breaks out into open revolt. The ruling classes are overthrown and the oppressed classes emancipated. But, as the new order emerges, new classes, new conditions of oppression, and new forms of struggle come into existence. And, when the forces of production change again, the new objective contradiction is resolved by its subjective counterpart in the class struggle. Following each change in the economic foundation of society, the superstructure undergoes a more or less rapid transformation so as to better serve the new order.

In Marx's theory, the state, religion, education, and propa-

ganda have an important role in the superstructure. The state,
according to Marx, first appeared when society began dividing
into classes. It can take a variety of forms: it can be a monarchy
or an aristocratic republic or even a democratic republic. But
whatever form it takes, as long as there are exploiters and exploited, it remains essentially the same. Except for some
periods when the state acquires a kind of independence of its
own, its executive committee is nothing but a committee of
men whose main task in life is to administer the consolidated
affairs of the classes that dominate the economic process.
Being the political expression of the social system, the state is
intrinsically coercive (and not, as Hegel had believed, society
become rational). It represses anything that challenges the prevailing order and uses the army, the bureaucracy, the secret
police, the judiciary, and censorship in order to fulfil its function. Put in another way, the political power of the state is the
organized use of force to enable those who own the means of
production to rule by compelling those who own only their
labour power — and who represent the vast majority of society
— to work systematically for them and to subject themselves
to the laws and regulations that are being promulgated. As
long as the historical evolutionary pattern demands division of
labour and private property, the state has a place in the social
order. But, when there is no longer any need for coercion, the
state will wither away because it alienates from man his political powers which he must exercise in order to develop himself
fully.

According to Marx, because of the revolutionary changes
that must take place in society each time the modes of production change, there is no such thing as an eternal and universal principle of right or wrong. There is only "class morality" — and each epoch must generate its own ethics. Therefore, religion is merely a political instrument that wears a spiritual mask. Being part of the superstructure, it justifies the
domination and interests of the ruling class. But, apart from
sanctifying the established order, it has the role of comforting
and providing spiritual compensation to those who are being
exploited. Because it promises a heaven and eternal salvation
to those who must suffer their fate on earth, Marx described

religion as "the sigh of the oppressed creature, the heart of a heartless world, and the spirit of spiritless conditions. It is the opium of the people." He rejected atheism as something irrelevant. Religion, like the state, will fade away when the order of society based on division of labour and private property no longer exists. It will have lost its functions.

Education and propaganda are directed towards indoctrinating the people with prejudices that serve the interests of the ruling class because each "class which puts itself in the place of the one ruling before it, is compelled, merely in order to carry through its aims, to represent its interests as the common interest of all the members of society, put in an ideal form; it will give its ideas the form of universality, and represent them as the only rational universally valid ones". Thus, because the class that has the means of material production at its disposal has control at the same time over the means of mental production and the distribution of ideas, the ideas and values of the ruling class become the ruling ideas and the main intellectual force. As a result, man's consciousness is not an original "pure" consciousness but a social product reflecting his existence in a particular social order.

As the antagonism between the historically decisive classes creates the conflict that makes the revolutionary transformation of society possible, the class struggle is the driving force of history. It is the inner essence of the historical progression Marx believed would lead to the eventual emancipation of mankind and, therefore, is the key to Marx's theory. (This is yet another departure from the ideas of Hegel, who regarded the state, and not a social class, as the agent of change in society.)

The next two sections of this chapter outline how in Marx's theory the capitalist order develops but gradually the "capitalist cloak becomes a straitjacket" when the "monopoly of capital becomes a fetter upon the mode of production". At some stage the dispossessed masses, whether they are aware of it yet or not, will overthrow the system. They will seize all the means of production from the capitalists and turn them into public property. Having abolished private property, the existing anarchy of production will be replaced by a consciously planned production for the common good. Gradually man, in free collaboration with all others, will develop the productive processes to a stage at which he will be able to leave the realm of necessity and enter the realm of freedom. Everyone will receive according to his or her needs and will be given opportunities to become a whole human being. The communist society that will have come into being is the final stage in the evolutionary process.

The Growth and Decline of the Capitalist System

While Marx was working on his ideas, Western Europe was passing through the turmoil created by the transition to the industrial age. It is only natural that the role and destiny of the emerging "capitalist system" should be the subject of the bulk of his writings. His major work, *Capital*, is primarily a critique of production during the capitalist epoch.

The coming into being of the capitalist system is described in the previous section. In Marx's evolutionary design it has the historic task of accumulating capital — that is, of bringing about industrialization. Marx was greatly impressed by the "unheard-of" development of the productive forces and, in the *Communist Manifesto*, wrote:

> The bourgeoisie, during its rule of scarce one hundred years, has created more massive and more colossal productive forces than have all preceding generations together. Subjection of nature's forces to man, machinery, application of chemistry to industry and agriculture, steam navigation, railways, electric telegraphs, clearing of whole continents for cultivation, canalisation of rivers, whole populations conjured out of the ground — what earlier century had even a presentiment that such productive forces slumbered in the lap of social labour?

Also, by creating great cities capitalism had "rescued a considerable part of the population from the idiocy of rural life". It had made the country dependent on the town, replacing the feudal dependency of the town of the country. But Marx was fully conscious that capitalism was putting an end to the certainties of traditional society by destroying the comparative security and self-sufficiency of the feudal community. The sense of belonging that was part of village life was being replaced by loneliness and despair. Labourers were forced to live in miserable conditions around the factories in which they worked and in which they were ruthlessly exploited. Their misery and alienation, he prophesied, would increase and force them into developing a revolutionary class-consciousness. As a result, the capitalist system would survive only until it had created the productive capacity required to enable the workers to free themselves from bondage.

Now let us see how Marx expected this to come about.

As described earlier, in capitalist society the class conflict was evolving between the capitalist class — which Marx referred to as the "bourgeoisie", and the working class — which he referred to as the "proletariat". *Bourgeois* was the name applied in French towns to a person belonging to the middle class — that is, a member of the community (apart from the landowners) who had property and therefore owned and controlled the means of production. The proletariat, who in ancient Rome were the citizens without property and assured income, are, in the Marxian theory, the class of people who depend entirely on the proceeds of the sale of their labour power for their livelihood. Marx was aware that social classes, being the product of historical development, are neither homogeneous nor unchangeable and that there are degrees in the social structure. This did not affect his analysis; as already mentioned, what mattered was the relationship of the classes to the means of production. The bourgeoisie owns the means of production (but needs the labour power of the proletariat because the means of production are useless unless labour is applied to them) and the proletariat does not own property (and therefore depends on the bourgeoisie to secure the necessities of life). The "middle and intermediate strata" that obliterate the lines of demarcation between the two "decisive and historically determining classes" in capitalist society are merely transition classes that wither away, leaving society polarized into two great hostile camps.

Each class is split into various factions in line with the division of labour, and there is even strong antagonism among the members of each faction because they must compete with each other in the market. Nevertheless, the common element always comes to the fore to carry on the battle against the other class. The only real link between the two opposing classes is sordid cash payments. And, because the modes of production require the exploitation of the proletarian masses by the bourgeoisie, the state — as in the past when it served the needs of the absolute monarch or the nobility — is little else but the servant of the capitalist class.

According to Marx, a fundamental difference between the capitalist and the preceding systems is that capitalism is founded on the pursuit of crude self-interest. Everything is based on selfish calculations appropriate to an economic system built on a universal unshackled competitive struggle. This "free competition" is not confined to the producers of goods who must compete for customers; it is also forced upon the workers who must compete for each job. The ability to work — labour power — is just another commodity to be negotiated for money. Nothing escapes competition's embrace: virtue, love, conviction, conscience, and the like all pass into commerce and become an object of exchange — to be bought and sold. Because everyone and everything is exposed to the vicissitudes of competition and to all the fluctuations in the market, there is "everlasting uncertainty and agitation", and this distinguishes the bourgeois epoch from all the earlier ones.

The industrial capitalists are forced to charge low — that is, competitive — prices, and because of it they must strive to keep their costs down. As labour is the major cost item in production, the first thing the capitalists do is to try to reduce wages to a level barely enough to enable their workers to survive and reproduce in sufficient number to provide replacements when they, not unlike the machines they serve, are worn out. In addition, because the profit margin on each unit produced must be low, the capitalists, wishing to survive, must produce greater quantities. In other words, they strive not only to reduce wages to their minimum but also to increase working hours to their maximum. And, to make this possible, the capitalists create an industrial "reserve army" — a pool of unemployed workers who, by waiting at factory gates, make those inside realize that they are expendable and as a consequence without any bargaining power.

But, in order to produce greater and greater quantities at competitive prices while — at the same time — ensuring the continuous existence of a reserve of potential workers outside their gates, the industrial capitalists must constantly strive to raise productivity — that is, the average output per man-hour worked. They achieve this by investing more and more of their profits in the development of new productive techniques and in labour-saving machinery. .This constant accumulation of productive capacity forced upon the capitalists by competition raises the potential to produce more and more goods. And, as already mentioned, this is the historic task and justification for the existence of the capitalist system. In fact, the term *capitalist system* popularized by Marx implies no more than a system that is built on the accumulation and use of capital.

In the long run, Marx contended, this growing capacity to produce would create conditions that would allow a better life for mankind; but, in the meantime — that is, while the capitalist system subsisted — it would lead to an intensification of the exploitation of the working class, to alienation, to monopolization, and to ever-worsening economic crises. It would lead to a state of permanent stagnation amidst a sea of misery, and eventually to the collapse of the whole civilization into barbarity, if the capitalist system were not destined to be overthrown before this happened.

The rest of this section describes how Marx expected all this to come about.

Marx's concept of "exploitation" is an extension of the "labour theory of value" propounded by David Ricardo (1773-1823). Ricardo was one of the most eminent of the classical school of British economists. He held that the value of a commodity (value is something quite different from price, which, while related to value, is set in the market by the relationship between demand and supply) depends on the relative quantity of labour required in its production. Marx seized upon this theory and, in a manner that would have surprised Ricardo had he been still alive, incorporated it into his design.

If the value of a commodity depends upon the quantities of human labour embodied in it, Marx argued, then this value rightfully belongs to those who have laboured to produce it. It follows, if the worker labours ten hours a day and for the pay he receives he can "buy back" only four hours' worth of what he has produced, then he has been cheated of what he has produced in the other six hours. He is denied the full and rightful benefits of his labour. Marx called the labour of the four hours "socially necessary labour" and that involved in the other six hours "surplus labour". The output of surplus labour he described as "surplus output" or "surplus value" because it went to the capitalist, who was not entitled to it.

Surplus value included not only the profits the producing capitalist made himself but also the amounts he had to part with in order to pay other capitalists rent and interest. Marx argued that rent and interest payments were part of surplus value because all productive assets belonged to the people. Land and mineral resources were provided by nature, and as long as no labour was applied to them they had no value whatsoever and should not be paid for. Factories, machines, tools, and so on, were nothing but "accumulated labour" — labour converted into productive assets. In the past someone had laboured to produce them instead of producing something for immediate consumption. In short, capital being the product of labour, or labour in disguise, the capitalist was not justified in paying rent for, or interest on, the capital he used to someone who has not laboured to produce it.

This idea of a surplus value is the theoretical foundation on which much of Marx's economic analysis of all systems based on the division into classes is built. The essential difference between them "lies only in the mode in which surplus labour is in each case extracted from the actual producer, the labourer". "Surplus value" is little more than pure abstraction and, from the economic point of view, even negative in value; but morally it sounds right and politically it is potent. The contention that all assets have already been paid for by past labour also gives theoretical justification to Marx's demand for common ownership of all existing property. The notion of a surplus value enabled Marx to write about a "rate of exploitation" of the workers by relating the amount of surplus value to that of wages: the rate of exploitation equals surplus value divided by the wages earned in producing it. Wages do not have to fall to raise the level of exploitation; in fact, they can even increase. It is enough for surplus value to rise at a faster rate than the wages earned while producing it — that is, while workers are being paid more and their standard of living is rising, the rate of their exploitation is still increasing. A greater proportion of what they are producing is being exproppriated by the capitalists.

Despite Marx's rhetoric of "naked, shameless, direct, and brutal exploitation", he did not really mean by the term *exploitation* an ethical condemnation. He did not equate exploitation with robbing. He merely described the relationship between the capitalists and the workers created by the requirements of the productive process during the capitalist stage. To be able to sell his output at competitive prices, Marx said, the capitalist must continuously appropriate from his workers surplus value — or "unpaid labour" — to be in the position to acquire labour-saving productive assets. Because of the coercion, by forces external to himself, constantly to extend and improve his productive assets in order to raise the productivity of his workers, the capitalist is no less the prisoner of the system than is the worker he is exploiting. In other words, the system is not unjust within its own rules and the capitalist performs a social function because, by accumulating capital, he creates the preconditions for a better society.

Apart from the need for greater output, asserted Marx, a capitalist must use his machines to the full because not to do so is a loss to him. They rust and they become obsolescent. As machines never tire, the capitalist will try to extend the working day even further and to intensify the work of the workers either by speeding up the pace of the machines or by tightening discipline. This forces the worker to pour in more and more energy, and, as a result, he ages more quickly. Moreover, as machines dispense with the need for muscular power, more and more women and children are employed. Since income need be only high enough to support a family on the subsistence level, employing the whole family makes it possible to appropriate a great deal more labour time for the same amount of wages.

But, as stressed above, Marx was in favour of machines as such. Modern technology was not here to enslave man but was the means to liberate him. The less time society required to produce the necessities of life, the more time it would have to engage in other forms of production—material and intellectual. However, de decried the way in which machines had to be used during the capitalist stage of the historical development in order to extract more and more surplus value from the workers.

As described in the previous section, Marx's basic premise was that it was in the nature of man to be a self-determining and creative being, and that man had a need to develop his human potentials in order to realize himself as a "whole" man. Marx regarded the constraints imposed on man by the capitalist system that deny him his right to fulfil himself as its fundamental evil. Under no other social order was man's degradation and alienation so thoroughgoing and so complete.

Man is dissociated from the product of his labour, Marx said. He plays no part in deciding what he makes and what becomes of it afterwards. He cannot use his product to keep alive or to engage in further activity. According to Marx, man puts something of himself into what he produces and, because his product does not belong to him, the more he produces the poorer he becomes — less and less is left of himself. And, by being in service, man does not belong to himself but to someone else. He is told where, when, and how to work. The living being is reduced to the status of an object: a tool of production bought and sold in the market.*

The introduction of machinery and mass production, the demand for efficiency, and other aspects that characterize the capitalist system, Marx claimed, were developing the division

---

* Marx regarded money as an absolute moral evil. It was the means by which men were turned into commodities. Because money manipulated both man's product and his activity, instead of man dominating both, man had lost control over his destiny. And, because money — or price — was the standard by which everything was valued, including man's labour, man was robbed of his proper worth.

of labour to such a degree that it had become the major contributing factor in alienation. At an ever-increasing rate man was being alienated from his productive activity, form his human powers, and from his fellow men.

Man was alienated from his productive activity by being turned into an ignorant tool and appendage to machines. He was dominated by dead matter; he had to follow the movement of machines instead of dictating to them. Because the traditional relationship of the craftsman to his tools was destroyed, productive activity had lost all semblance of self-activity and any charm it may have possessed. It only expressed man's powerlessness and the reality of his inhuman existence. At work, man felt homeless, physically exhausted, and mentally depressed. He only worked to secure the means necessary for his subsistence and, when there was no compulsion, work was avoided like the plague.

Because only the simplest, most monotonous, and most easily acquired skills were expected of him, the worker could not develop himself in his work. He was trapped in a particular sphere of repetitive activity, and conditioned to act and think within the confines of his specialized role. In short, he was alienated from the opportunity for creative and spontaneous labour so necessary for him to express his species powers — that is, the distinctive capacities that separate the human from all other species.

The division into social classes — an aspect of all societies that have resorted to division of labour — alienates man from his fellow men, Marx said. Individuals have come to regard themselves and others as being in socially imposed and artificial categories, and not as equals. They conform to social rules that are independent of their will. This renders most forms of free co-operation and a reciprocal communal life impossible. Marx wrote that, in capitalist society, social relations "are not relations between individual and individual, but between worker and capitalist, between farmer and landlord, and so on".

And alienation affects not only the worker but also the propertied classes — though to a much lesser extent. To them, at least, life still has the appearance of a human existence.

Nevertheless, their advantages are relative rather than absolute because, as already mentioned, they too are forced to play a role within the economic system that is independent of their will. They are as much under the control of the market with respect to what to produce, what prices to set, and what happens to their products as the workers are under their control. Being "theoretically" and not "practically" connected with production, the capitalists are denied the direct working relationship to production which Marx believed to be so essential for human fulfilment. Moreover, the capitalists have their social relations restricted. Because the workers cannot have human relations with them, they cannot have human relations with the workers. Nor can the capitalists freely relate to those within their own class because they have to compete with one another in the market place.

As capitalism matures, society polarizes into a small number of capitalists and the huge mass of proletarians. Former tradesmen and other small producers (together with the shopkeepers and small peasants with whom they form the lower strata of the middle class) are unable to compete with machine-produced goods. This is partly because their capital is insufficient to produce at the scale on which modern industry is conducted and partly because their specialized skills are rendered worthless by the new modes of production. Gradually they are dispossessed and, being left with nothing but their labour power to acquire life's subsistence, sink into the proletariat. This decline of the middle class is inevitable because, by representing small-scale production, it is merely a relic from the feudal system and an anachronism in a mass-production society.

As mentioned earlier, Marx said that the capitalist, in order to keep his prices down so that he can compete in the market, accumulates more and more labour-saving capital, and this leads to higher and higher labour productivity; that is, output per worker rises. The result is that the more capital they accumulate, the fewer workers they employ in relation to the capital assets being used. This in turn means that the income of the workers, in relation to output, falls further and further behind. Since the workers represent the vast majority of the people, the higher output cannot be sold at the current prices. Because the capitalists must reduce prices in order to sell their output, the average rate of return on capital invested — despite some fluctuations in specific commodities — continuously falls.* As time passes, many capitalists cease to be able to continue accumulating additional capital. While some capitalists merge their assets, others who are less efficient or less ruthless are expropriated and forced to join the proletariat.

As the number of the capitalists contracts and the means of production concentrate in fewer and fewer hands, competition — the basic driving force of the capitalist system — is gradually strangled. Monopolies, in the form of trusts, cartels, and the like, develop. Only huge aggregates are strong enough to withstand the fall in the rate of profit. Moreover, the emerging joint stock companies have the tendency to separate the function of management from that of ownership; paid managers replace the capitalists who, as a result, become more and more superfluous. There arises a new aristocracy of finance, of promoters, and of merely nominal directors, who create a whole system of swindling and cheating by means of company promotions, stock jobbing, and the like. Instead of accumulating new capital assets and watching the rate of return decline further, they buy up all new inventions and prohibit their utilization. The system ceases to progress: the point is reached where the forces of production have outgrown the capitalist mode of production and the existing class relations are only so many fetters that must be burst asunder.

Throughout its existence, Marx said, the capitalist system, unlike any previous society, would be plagued by periodic expansions and contractions in the scale of accumulation, production, and employment. They would result from its unplanned and unregulated operation in which independent units

* For example if a capitalist has invested, say, $100,000 in his business and if he makes $10,000 profit in a year then his rate of return on the capital invested equals 10 per cent. If he adds another $100,000 to the capital already invested — that is, his total capital in the business is increased to $200,000 — and his profit rises to $15,000 then his rate of return equals 7.5 per cent. This means that, despite an increase in his profits, the rate of return on the capital used has fallen.

produce for profits and not in response to social needs. (This concept of economic cycles — known to us as business or trade cycles: booms and depressions — is regarded as one of Marx's outstanding contribution to economic theory.) His reasoning was as follows: when a special stimulus, such as opening of new markets or developing new social wants, brings about a sudden expansion of industry, there is an increase in the demand for labour that is met by drawing on the industrial reserve army. As the size of the reserve army decreases and a shortage of labour develops, the bargaining power of the workers improves and they force wages up. The capitalists, in order to countervail the decline in the reserve army, accelerate the rate at which they accumulate labour-saving machinery. The outcome is that productivity increases and fewer workers are needed, and, as the number in the reserve army rises, wages slip back to their previous level. This reduces the purchasing power of the proletariat. The overall effect is that, at least in some staple commodities, there is overproduction in relation to demand — though not in relation to the real needs of the people. Because the masses with their low wages cannot buy all that is being produced, there is overproduction which has its roots in underconsumption. As Marx puts it: "The ultimate reason for all real crises always remains the poverty and restricted consumption of the masses."

During the crisis, the capitalists, because they cannot sell all they produce, destroy a great part of the previously created productive capacity, conquer new markets, and more thoroughly exploit the old ones. Eventually, the rate of profit is restored to its former level and the economy settles down to a new equilibrium. There is a new impulse to accumulate capital in order to produce cheaper goods and thus increase the level of profits. The equilibrium lasts until once again some special stimulus precipitates an overproduction of capital that leads to an overproduction of goods and a new crisis.

As time passes, the constant accumulation and concentration intensify capital's inherent tendency towards overproduction. As a result, each successive crisis is more destructive and all-embracing than the previous one. It puts on trial, each time more thoroughly, the existence of the entire capitalist society. This capitalist society "that has conjured up such gigantic means of production and of exchange, is like the sorcerer who is no longer able to control the powers of the nether world that he has called up by his spells". In the end there is a final crisis when the system is overthrown by the proletariat. Material privation and spiritual oppression will have compelled it to liberate itself.

As discussed at some length, Marx had brought what he believed to be "scientific" proof of an evolutionary historical process in which a progression of social orders have a defined role to play. His analysis of the capitalist system shows how it fulfils its historic role of industrialization (as far as this is possible within the capitalist system) and of creating a class-conscious proletariat which will bring about its downfall.

Marx's interpretation of the forces working within society made him, a fundamentally humanist philosopher, accept the idea that there was a need for violence and bloodshed because the capitalist would not step aside without a fight. Despite some hesitation later in his life (which may have been merely a tactical move), he believed that revolution was the "midwife of progress". The supremacy of the capitalists had to be wrested from them by a proletarian revolution and "not only because the ruling class cannot be overthrown in any other way, but also because only in a revolution can the class which overthrows it rid itself of the accumulated rubbish of the past and become capable of reconstructing society".

Although somewhat ambiguous on the subject and confused by rhetoric, Marx seems to have been concerned with the timing of the revolutionary transformation. While nothing could shake his conviction that the bourgeois world was destined for destruction and that the victory of the proletariat was inevitable, he knew that man could advance or delay the revolution. It should not come before the capitalists had completed their part in the process of industrialization, because a victory would be only a temporary one: "No social order even disappears before all the productive forces for which there is room in it have been developed; and new higher relations of production never appear before the material conditions of their existence have matured in the womb of the old society." But the revolution should take place once the existing relations had outgrown their usefulness and were becoming fetters upon new forces of production — otherwise the workers would be the victims of rapidly intensifying misery without good cause. He must have had this in mind when he so passionately championed the working class and strove to develop its political awareness so that it would be ready to take over when the time was ripe.

Marx saw the proletarian revolution as the climax in a developing pattern. At the outset, the workers are an incoherent mass of runaway serfs, dispossessed peasants, poverty-stricken artisans, beggars and vagrants. As time passes — owing to the technical organization of the factories in which machines erase all distinction of status, work, and pay among the workers, and in which they suffer ever-increasing exploitation and alienation — the workers become aware of their common situation and their special interests. Gradually they remould themselves, learn to combine and to develop an integrated proletarian class-conscious purpose of their own. Instead of just being a "class in itself", they become a "class for itself" — that is, a class not only conscious of its moral and physical poverty but a class also aware of its historically ordained goal.

At first the fight is carried on by individual labourers, then by the workpeople of a factory, then by the operatives of one trade in one locality, against the individual capitalist who directly exploits them. At this stage they form an incoherent mass scattered over the whole country and broken up by mutual competition. They waste their strength on seemingly foolish and futile acts. They smash the machines they operate, set ablaze the factories in which they work, or destroy the imported wares that compete with what they produce. Now and then they are victorious — but only for a time. While the riots are drowned in blood, their real fruit lies in the ever-expanding union of the workers. As time passes, thanks to the modern means of communication which enable workers in different localities to maintain contact with one another, all the local struggles become centralized into a national struggle between the two classes. And as the workers' strength grows, they feel that strength more. While the organization of the proletariat is repeatedly upset by the continuing competition between the workers themselves, "it ever rises again, stronger, firmer, mightier".

This progress of the proletariat is assisted from the outside in a number of ways. Their leadership is strengthened by those capitalists who fall by the wayside during the industrial concentration, and also by a portion of the bourgeois ideologists (no doubt meaning people like himself and Engels) who, comprehending theoretically the historical movement as a whole, join them and "supply the proletariat with fresh elements of enlightenment and progress".

As the scattered production units are being concentrated more and more in large aggregates, masses of labourers are agglomerated around factories and mines, and organized like soldiers. An industrial army of workmen, under the command of a capitalist, requires, like a real army, officers (managers) and sergeants (foremen) who exercise authority on behalf of the capitalist during the labour process. This teaches the workers how to organize themselves into disciplined, unified, and well-integrated armies.

Moreover, the bourgeoisie must again and again turn to the proletariat to fight its battles. First with the aristocracy, later with those portions of the bourgeoisie whose interests become antagonistic to the progress of industry, and at all times with the bourgeoisie of foreign countries. The capitalist must compete with his counterpart in other countries as the "need of a constantly expanding market for its products chases the bourgeoisie over the whole surface of the globe. It must nestle everywhere, settle everywhere, establish connections everywhere."

As economic crises worsen, capitalism moves into its final crisis. The proletariat, having acquired a class-consciousness and an awareness of its historic mission, makes the revolution. The capitalists have produced their own grave diggers. "The knell of capitalist private property sounds. The expropriators are expropriated."

To sum up, Marx believed the capitalists were doomed by the inevitable logic of the development of the productive forces. They were forced not only to forge the weapons for their own destruction but also to call into existence the men to wield these weapons — the proletarians. But, by the time the revolution took place, the capitalist order would have fulfilled its destiny: it would have created the material conditions and developed the proletariat sufficiently not only to bring to an end the prehistoric stage of human society — the divided society, but also to usher in the ultimate order.

The Communist Society

Marx held that nobody can foresee exactly how a future society will be organized. He viewed himself as an interpreter of an evolutionary historical pattern, but believed that neither is one able nor is there a need to solve the problems of the future. As he refused to make dogmatic predictions, he left no blueprint of the nature of the communist society. In fact, Marx had very little to say on this subject. Nevertheless, especially in his early writings, one can gain a glimpse of what he expected it to be like.

Because, after the overthrow of the capitalist system, society would be "in every respect, economically, morally, and intellectually, still stamped with the birthmarks of the old society from whose womb it emerges", there would have to be two distinct phases. The first phase Marx saw as the "dictatorship of the proletariat". This would be a transitional phase between the capitalist and the communist society, in which there would be a revolutionary transformation of the one into the other. This stage — to which Marx also referred as the "first phase of communism" and "socialism" — may be said to be part of the revolution. In the second phase, true "communism" — meaning the realm of freedom and reason the young Marx had craved for — would come to prevail. This post-capitalist order is discussed below.

The revolution would have raised the proletariat to the position of ruling class, and during the dictatorship of the proletariat, it would impose its supremacy. The state would continue to exist and to be used as an organ of coercion. To reiterate, Marx did not regard the state as an instrument that promoted the general welfare of the community: it primarily represented political power, which was the organized power of one class to dominate the other. But, instead of being a bourgeois state oppressing the workers, it would be a proletarian state — meaning a democratic state in the sense that the proletariat are the immense majority of the population — which would gradually wrest the instruments of production, distribution, and exchange from the capitalists and centralize them in its hands. At first, banking, the means of communication, transport, and the large landed estates would be confiscated, and wholesale commerce and foreign trade would become a state monopoly. But small business would be untouched, because it would be futile to think that all private property could be abolished at a stroke.

As explained earlier, Marx assumed that at the time of the proletarian revolution all productive forces — capital and labour — would have reached an advanced stage. To assist their development to full capacity, and also to ensure a more equitable distribution of what was being produced, a centralized planning authority would begin operating. Man would cease to be subordinated to unmastered forces. The anarchy of capitalist production would be replaced by a socially planned regulation of production in accordance with the needs of society as a whole.

During the dictatorship of the proletariat, while everyone would be under an equal obligation to work, people would not be paid according to their needs but according to their skills and the intensity and duration of their work. The resulting inequality would be levelled down by a vigorously graduated income tax — that is, a tax levied in such a manner that, as income rose, proportionally more and more would be taken away by way of tax. Nobody would be paid interest, and all rents would be applied to public purposes. Everything an individual received would be in return for his labour and nothing else, and all that he could acquire would be for consumption only. In addition, all rights to inheritance would be abolished. Thus, no man would be in the position to accumulate property.

Money would be abolished. A worker would receive a nontransferable certificate that he had furnished such and such amount of labour. After deductions had been made for his labour for the common good, he would be able to acquire, from the social stock, consumption goods whose production would have involved the same amount of labour — and, therefore, had the same value — as he had produced.

The means of propaganda, such as the press, would be subject to working class direction. So would education, which would be free to all children. Having been rescued from the influence of the bourgeois class, education would be combined with material production. It would produce a generation capable of establishing communism. Instead of turning out a mere fragment of a man, it would turn out a "fully developed individual, fit for a variety of labour, ready to face any change of production, and to whom the different social functions he performs are but so many modes of giving free scope to his own natural and acquired powers".

After the final victory of the proletariat — that is, when the entire bourgeois class and all other vestiges of capitalism had been abolished — the proletariat would have eliminated its supremacy as it would have no other class to dictate to. In fact, it would have destroyed its own entity: there would be no such thing as a proletarian or any other class left. The state would wither away because in a classless society there is no need for political power. Truly free men need no rules imposed from above laying down what needs to be done and what should not be done. There would be democracy spreading from below to the top. All posts — administrative, judicial, and so on — would be filled on the basis of universal suffrage of all concerned and subject to recall at any time by the same electors. All officials, whatever their position, would receive the same amount of goods and services as all other workers. The communist society would have come into existence. It would be the final stage in the historical progression, as there would be no class struggle to be resolved by the establishment of a new order.

With the means of production under the control of the workers, and freed from the fetters of capitalist profit calculations, man would co-operate freely with other men. He would know that only in association with others could he cultivate his talents and fully develop his creative and productive potentials. The place of work would become a community of free individuals carrying on their work in such a manner that the labour power of all the different individuals would be consciously applied as the combined labour power of the whole group. Machines would be the servants of men instead of being their masters. As a result, tasks would be accomplished with the least expenditure of energy, and in such conditions as is proper and worthy of human beings. Labour, instead of being an activity to which one was condemned in order to survive, would become an activity worth while in itself. A burden would be turned into a source of self-fulfilment and enjoyment.

Because in the communist society possession would not be the "unique goal of life and existence", the relation between man and woman would become a natural relation of love instead of being one of ownership and dominance. The relation of man to woman being the most natural relation of human being to human being, love would exchange for love and not for money. Women would no longer be another form of exclusive private property occupying the position of mere instruments of reproduction. The family would cease to be an affair of money in which children were exploited by their parents and transformed into articles of commerce and tools of labour. And, by giving each individual the scope he needs in society in order to develop his life to its full potential, the social conditions that engender crime and create beggars, drunkards, and hooligans would be removed.

Religion would lose its purpose as the system would require no moral justification and the masses would need no spiritual consolation. In fact, according to Marx, it would show a defect in the system if there were no "emancipation from religion"; the conditions that required religion would have not been fully eliminated. As all private property in land would be abolished, land would no longer be the object of sordid speculation. The intimate relationship of man to land would thus be restored and, through freedom of work and enjoyment, land would once again be the real property of man. Industrial and agricultural armies would make it possible for industry to be decentralized and for waste land to be brought under cultivation.

Thus the subjection of the country to the rule of the city would fade away and all distinction between the two would disappear.

In communist society there would be no conflict between the interests of the community and those of the individual. The social administration, elected through universal suffrage, would watch over the interests of both society and each individual. Allowances would be made for differences in individual physical and mental endowments that make it possible for one person to supply more labour in the same time or to labour for longer periods. Society would also allow for one worker being married, another not, one having more children than another, and so on.

When the individual is no longer coerced by necessity to work in order to survive, his enslaving subordination to the division of labour would vanish. Instead of having an exclusive sphere of activity allotted to him, man would be able to choose his activity freely. He would have the means of cultivating his gifts in all directions and become accomplished in any branch he wished. In the communist society there would be no painters but, at most, people who engaged in painting among other things. Man would hunt, fish, or raise cattle, without becoming a hunter, a fisherman, or a cattleman.

Towards the end of his life Marx added leisure as another choice man would have. Because there would be no need to produce surplus value for an exploiting class, working hours would be reduced to the necessary minimum. According to Marx, the amount of free time available to all members of society is the true measure of a nation's wealth, because disposable time enables each individual not only to enjoy more leisure but also to increase his education in the arts, the sciences, and so on.

Throughout, and with undiminishing fervour, Marx was idealistic in his belief in the "truly human" society. He entertained no doubt whatsoever that the working class, when in power, would act reasonably and justly to bring about a society without classes and rulers. He never wavered in his conviction that men, after eliminating all that alienates them — corruption, competition, and externally imposed occupational roles and class categories — would fully co-operate with one another. In this free association, they would rationally regulate their exchange with nature, control the social conditions of their lives so that "the free development of each is the condition of the free development of all", and create the basis for "rendering it impossible that anything should exist independent of individuals". In this environment, each man would manifest and enrich his multi-sided human powers and develop into what he had the capacity to become. This "whole", "universal" individual would display physical and mental flexibility that would surpass anything believed possible before. And when, thanks to the all-round development of each individual, all the springs of co-operative wealth flowed abundantly and satisfied all the real needs of man, society would inscribe on its banners: "From each according to his ability, to each according to his needs".

Marx wrote that socialist societies would be established within national boundaries at different times because "no social order ever disappears before all the productive forces for which there is room have developed; and new, higher relations of production never appear before the material conditions of their existence have matured in the womb of the old society". As each country first had to develop under the capitalist system until the time was ripe for the revolutionary transfer of the ownership of the means of production to the people, those countries that established a socialist society earlier would have the role of being models, and also the bases, for the revolution in other countries.

But the revolution would spread rapidly because the capitalists would transform the whole world into their image. Owing to the immensely facilitated means of communication, the vast improvement of all instruments of production would draw even the most barbaric nations into civilization. Nobody would be able to resist the temptation to acquire cheap goods and this would compel all countries, on pain of extinction, to accept the capitalist system.

In the end there would be universal communism based upon the solidarity of the workers of the world. Just as one man would have stopped exploiting another, so one country would stop exploiting the other. There would be social justice, harmonious collaboration, and perpetual peace in a world of one faith. And man would enjoy not only freedom but also the ''all-sided production of the whole earth''.

3

Marxism as Political Ideology

As is discussed in the last chapter of this book, Marx's theory is today refutable on logical as well as factual grounds — but its impact on the minds of men is incalculable. The use of the Marxian conception as a tool in achieving social change has re-channelled the course of history, and history still continues to be made in its name. It has provided desperately needed theoretical backing to activists wishing to create a different political and social order from the one existing. The purpose of this chapter is to describe this impact.

Before the First World War

During the period when Marx was working on his ideas, labour was ruthlessly used, disfranchised, and living under miserable conditions. The economic thinkers of the day only spread gloom. They had reached the conclusion that the general standard of living could not be raised and, therefore, the masses would always remain close to subsistence level. People would have only enough to keep alive. Life, being a constant competitive struggle for survival, caused some to perish and allowed a few to lift themselves above the subsistence level. The wealthy were only the lucky few who managed to escape from grinding poverty. This promise of a future full of deprivation prompted the essayist and historian Thomas Carlyle, a contemporary of Marx, to describe economics as the dismal science. Into this world in which there seemed to be no release from misery, Marx, by assimilating the most diverse material and remoulding it, brought a message of hope: a prophecy of a land of freedom and plenty.

The publication of the *Communist Manifesto* in 1848 is hailed as having marked the beginning of the class struggle against the capitalists that would culminate in proletarian revolutions around the world. But, as already noted, this is rather an imaginative description of its immediate impact. At the time there was no indication of any concerted proletarian action. In fact, Marx's message was slow to take effect. But gradually the situation began to change. The economic crisis of 1857 resulted in the workers starting to shake off the apathy that had engulfed them since the fiasco of the 1848 revolutions. By the early 1860s they once again showed a tendency to organize and to call strikes. There was also a spirit of internationalism — more particularly among the English workers. The Polish revolt of 1863 against Russian occupation, which took more than a year to suppress and led to the intensification of repression, aroused much sympathy. In 1864, a meeting held in London attended by English, German, Italian, Swiss, and Polish workers — most of them exiles from their countries — decided to establish the International Working Men's Association. Today it is better known as the First International. Marx — after twelve years in which he kept aloof from political activity and consistently declined to associate himself with any sort of political organization — joined them as the representative of German artisans and was elected as one of the thirty-two members of its General Council.

Marx was invited to compose an "inaugural" address to the working classes. In his address, Marx called for the "eternal union of bortherly co-operation" of the whole militant working class of Europe and America. He stated that the organization "was founded in order to create a central means of unity and co-operation between the association of workers which already existed in various countries and aim at the same goal, namely, the protection, the rise, and the complete emancipation of the working class". In the spirit of the *Communist Manifesto*, he finished the address by calling the workers of the world to unite.

During the initial years of its activities, the First International functioned smoothly. Marx, who became the acknowledged leader of the General Council, had refrained from prescribing any definite way in which to conduct the struggle. Because of the heterogeneous nature of the organization, the statutes were so wide that it made it possible for the First International to accommodate all socialist views. Regular congresses formulated broad principles designed to guide members in their social and political battles but left it to the national sections to evolve their methods on the basis of the "real conditions" in their country. Marx refused to take part in several congresses because it interfered with his scientific work. Being its intellectual leader, he was more interested in the movement's historical role, while the main concern of each congress was with working hours, wage rates, working class education programmes, and the establishment of workers' co-operatives and credit unions. It supported strikes and negotiated between the trade unions of the various countries to help one another during a strike.

After the economic crisis of 1866-67, the First International was growing rapidly both in size and in prestige. It is estimated that, by the end of the 1860s, it had about eight hundred thousand dues-paying members. But dissent was soon to develop. One underlying cause of the differences of opinion was that many members advocated concerted world-wide revolutionary action, while Marx and his followers continued to press the view that world revolution had to be a step-by-step process. In each country the workers should settle matters with their respective bourgeoisie only when the material conditions, and the workers, were ready for the revolutionary transformation. Besides principles, there were other reasons for friction. Members had strong national and racial feelings, and, during the Franco-Prussian war, these asserted themselves.

After the defeat of France in 1871, the peace terms accepted by France seemed too humiliating to many Parisians. When government officials were moved to Versailles because the Prussians were at the gates of Paris, the void was filled by the Paris Commune, and hundreds of thousands of workers and members of the lower middle class took to the barricades. During the two months of the uprising, over seventeen thousand people — including women and children — were killed. Although the International had little to do with the uprising, and the General Council remained silent while it lasted, seventeen of the ninety-two members of the Council of the Commune were prominent members of the International.

Marx, who had urged the French workers to welcome the republic and not become involved in a rebellion that was bound to fail, was all along pessimistic about the Commune's chances of success. Nevertheless, three days after its collapse, he managed to make it an important part of the mythology of the Left by describing it as a turning point in the history of the working class. In an address, "The Civil War in France", he proclaimed: "The workingmen's Paris, with its Commune, will be for ever celebrated as the glorious harbinger of a new society", and that "the battle must break out again and again in ever-growing dimensions, and there can be no doubt as to who will be the victor in the end — the appropriating few, or the immense working majority."

Following his address, Marx was accused by a number of newspapers of having instigated the revolt in the first place. The hitherto virtually unknown Marx, having been presented as a potent menace to the established order, became widely known throughout Europe. A year later, a German edition of the *Communist Manifesto* was published.

But, by this time, despite his rhetoric, Marx seems to have given up all expectations of an early revolution. When, together with Engels, he wrote a short introduction to the German edition of the *Communist Manifesto* (it was short because, as they explained, its publication was too unexpected to give them much time to bridge the gap from 1847), it included the following significant statement: "However much the state of things may have altered during the last twenty-five years, the general principles laid down in the *Manifesto* are, on the whole, as correct today as ever. Here and there some detail may be improved. The practical application of the principles will depend, as the *Manifesto* itself states, everywhere and at all times, on the historical conditions for the time being existing, and, for that reason, no special stress is laid on the revolutionary measures proposed at the end of Section II. That passage would in many respects be differently worded today!" Marx had arrived at the conclusion that England, the United States and perhaps Holland were countries where the workers might be able to achieve their aims by peaceful means. This softening of the revolutionary doctrine introduced a new controversy over what was the best way of achieving working class emancipation, which fuelled the growing dissent within the International.

After the Paris Commune, the First International was a spent force. Its more moderate members were frightened off; the English, French, and Germans were losing interest, and it made progress only in Spain and Italy — which were strongholds of anarchism. Anarchism (the word derives from the Greek *anarkhos*, "without ruler") exerted a strong influence over radical thought, particularly in Russia and Latin countries — that is, in countries in which the state was always distrusted and regarded as something unnatural and artificially grafted on to society.

The anarchists laid great stress on the individual and asserted that the state restrained those natural impulses that made for harmony among men. The state had to be abolished and replaced by the free association of men in decentralized and self-governing communities in which neither private property nor religion was tolerated, women enjoyed full equality, marriage as an institution was abolished, and all children received free education. Only within a system in which there was complete freedom and equality could a stable order be achieved.

In the First International, the anarchists, under the leadership of Mikhail Bakunin, a Russian by birth, often clashed with the Marxists. They looked at machines as enslaving man and wanted a simple mode of production, while the Marxists advocated large-scale industrialization. Because they rejected all notions of any power being exercised by one man over other men, they rejected Marx's idea of a dictatorship of the proletariat. What they called "Marx's authoritarian communism" amounted to the replacement of one form of tyranny by another. Moreover, Marx strove to lead the workers as a whole — as a mass movement — into a revolution that would preserve much of what was good in the old one, and had laid down in 1850 that the working class should be told: "You

have to go through fifteen, twenty, fifty years of civil wars and
national struggles, not only in order to change conditions but
also to change yourselves and make yourself capable of political rule.'' Bakunin, on the other hand, believing that the
masses by instinct would build up life along the lines that
would be most suitable, wanted the complete annihilation of
the entire structure of society and the immediate triumph of
the workers. This was to be achieved by a highly conspiratorial
organization of disciplined professional revolutionaries, under
strong central control, who lived for nothing but to prepare for
the revolution. The object of the organization was "to use all
the means in its powers to intensify and spread suffering and
evil which must end by driving the people to revolt". To
Bakunin, everything that promoted the revolution was permissible and everything that hindered it was a crime. The conflict
between Marx and Bakunin made it very difficult for the First
International. In 1872, to escape control of the anarchists, the
headquarters of the General Council were transferred from
London to New York. For all practical purposes the First International ceased to exist, and it was formally dissolved in 1876.

Shortly after the move of the General Council to New
York, Marx retired from direct participation in organized activity. But, by this time — partly owing to the activities of the
First International which had encouraged a degree of working
class co-operation that had not existed before — his ideas had
begun to infiltrate, on a broad front, the minds of friend and
foe alike. After his death he came to be loved and revered by
millions, and the *Communist Manifesto* was translated into
every civilized language. He appealed even more to the educated than to the workers. The radical intellectuals became his
most ardent disciples. They treated his writings as if they were
scriptures, analysing them minutely and, when circumstances
demanded it, reading between the lines. Marx was the first to
provide them with a rationally integrated picture of the whole
social, economic, political, and cultural pattern of society,
which linked the past to the present and projected it into the
future. He had woven together the bewildering complexities of
human relations into one all-encompassing explanation.

The fact that Marx's doctrine is scattered throughout his

writings and that he had never summarized his thoughts into a coherent and integrated form facilitated the spread of his ideas. Even in his "scientific" work he was often obscure, careless in expression and inconsistent, giving ample scope to refinement and adjustments to various views and diverse circumstances. At any time Marxists (be they radical or moderate), non-Marxists, and anti-Marxists could — and still do — stress different parts of his work.

Marx's *Capital* is a massive work of 2,500 pages based on extensive research and acute reasoning: however, it is ill-organized, turgid in prose, and tortuous in its meaning. In addition to *Capital*, there are *The Economic and Philosophic Manuscripts of 1844, The Holy Family, German Ideology, Poverty of Philosophy, The Communist Manifesto, The Eighteenth Brumaire of Louis Bonaparte, Critique of the Gotha Programme*, plus pamphlets, essays, articles, and innumerable letters. Many of his writings were mere polemics with his contemporaries — in fact, he seems to have worked out some of his own ideas by way of attacking those of others. At times Marx assumed the role of agitator and radical organizer; the first demanding emotionalism, the second compromise. Like most other revolutionary thinkers, in some of his writings he adopted a passionate style in which he either violently exaggerated or grossly oversimplified his theories for the sake of being heard — and this further facilitated the varied interpretations of his theory.

The lack of cohesion can also be attributed to the fact that his literary work extended over forty eventful years and his ideas developed as time passed. Until about 1845, the young Marx was a humanitarian and ethical philosopher concerned primarily with alienation and the denial of man's free will. Between 1845 and 1849 he became a revolutionary activist who, with Engels, wrote the *Communist Manifesto*, in which they announced the inevitable destruction by revolution of the capitalist society and the abolition of private property, and edited the *Neue Rheinische Zeitung*, in which they urged the workers to take part in the revolution of 1848. After 1850, Marx began what he regarded as a "scientific" inquiry to find the laws that determine the way societies are organized and which govern social change through time. Within this scientific framework he was to elaborate what he had already proclaimed in the *Communist Manifesto.*

Between 1875 and 1890, the labour movement really began to take shape. Socialist parties and national trade unions were being organized in the industrializing countries in Western Europe. Invariably the Marxian concepts were incorporated into their ideology, providing them with a badly needed scientifically based programme. In 1889, when the Socialist International — that is, the Second International — was founded in Brussels, it formally accepted Marx's basic principles. The class struggle, international workers' solidarity, and the socialization of the means of production became its underlying philosophy. Thus Marx's ideas became the official creed of the whole organized international working-class movement. Marxism was well entrenched both as an intellectual force and as an ideology — and not only in Europe: it was taken by emigrants across the seas.

Unlike the First International, which was a loose association based on membership by individual trade unions and persons, the Second International was a federation of national working-class parties and trade unions. It held congresses every three years or so to which member organizations sent delegates. Their decisions regarding ideology, policies, and methods to be used were recognized by member organizations as coming from the highest authority. They represented Marxist orthodoxy to the world.

The Second International worked better than the First — at least on the surface. The greatest difficulty it had to cope with was that, at that time, the people of Europe had begun to reap the benefits of the Industrial Revolution, which had brought them so much suffering earlier. Because workers were enjoying a rising standard of living, many of its member organizations showed no desire for a revolutionary class struggle. Some had been admitted only because the Marxists expected to take full control of their members at the right time.

During this period the largest and best organized workers' party was the German Social Democratic Party. Since 1870, industrialization in Germany had proceeded at a very fast rate, and the number of the industrial workers increased in proportion. In the 1890 election, the party polled nearly a million and a half votes, which elected thirty-five of its candidates to the German parliament. This made the party a major force in the political life of the country, and its leaders became highly respected citizens. Despite divisions within its ranks — between the "revolutionaries", the "orthodox", and the "revisionists" — to the majority of the party the idea of revolution was accepted as ineviable in principle, but in the more immediate political sense it was merely a handy tool to extract concessions. Thus, notwithstanding its philosophy and its rhetoric, the party was a democratic socialist party wanting to establish socialism by evolutionary means within the existing order rather than by revolution. They saw no objection to working through the state instead of destroying it.

When other members of the Second International accused the German party of treating revolution as merely a theoretical policy, its leaders argued that all Marx really wanted was to improve the lot of the workers. If he had lived long enough to see the modern democratic state come into being — with its universal suffrage, general education, and redistribution of wealth through taxation — Marx would have changed his tactics. He would have opted for emancipation through trade unions and co-operatives and victory at the polls.* Marx would have recognized that there was no need to destroy the state because

---

* This seems doubtful, although, as mentioned before, later in his life Marx had toned down his emphasis on armed revolt. But, generally speaking, he believed that revolution was the midwife assisting in the birth of a new society that had formed in the womb of the old. In his major writings he had dismissed any idea that the capitalist state could be reformed and asserted that therefore it must be completely abolished. He condemned all experiments in social planning within the capitalist framework as being foredoomed to failure; they were merely calculated to weaken the revolutionary fervour of the masses. Democratic capitalist society was so contrived that the real power always remained in the hands of the dominant class and franchise only gave people the right to decide once every three or six years which member of the ruling class was to misrepresent them in parliament. He expected the bourgeoisie to suppress democratic institutions and workers' parties if their supremacy were really endangered — as indeed was to happen in Germany and elsewhere.

the state was nothing but a tool that operated in accordance with the wishes of the people who controlled it. It could be adapted not only for use in the interest of different classes but, eventually, also for use in a classless society. There was no reason why an instrument of class-coercion could not be transformed into an instrument of social service.

In Great Britain, which at the time was the most industrialized country in the world, Marxism had taken few roots despite the fact that it should have been the nearest to the historically predestined proletarian revolution. Marx, who had lived and worked most of his life in London, was practically unknown. The promotion of socialist ideals was mainly the work of the Fabian Society, which came into being in 1883 and later helped to found the British Labour Party to which it transferred much of its ideology. The Fabians were radical bourgeois liberals who accepted the idea of centralized control, because they believed that this would raise production, but repudiated the Marxist class struggle and refused to idealize the workers or to regard them as entrusted with a historical mission. Instead of revolution they wanted piecemeal social changes that would put such things as education, transport, mines, and most mass production of staple goods into the hands of a highly organized state. Although they were advocating nationalization, they did not seek the expropriation of all private property.

In France, after the Paris Commune of 1871, the workers had shed their traditional revolutionary zeal. They seem to have recognized the futility of revolution by way of street fights and barricades to capture state power and adopted a more gradual and peaceful form of political action. Moreover, as in the rest of Europe, poverty in France was not so much among the regular industrial workers whom Marx had counted upon to make the revolution because they had "nothing to lose but their chains", as among a class of people who could hardly be classed as workers. Marx had dismissed them as *Lumpenproletariat* — meaning down-and-out good-for-nothing social scum who were more likely to become the venal tools of the forces of reaction than to become entangled in the proletarian movement. As regards Marx's ideas, their interpretation by French "Marxists" was such that in 1882 Marx was to declare: "What is certain is that I am not a Marxist."

Developments were even less promising in the United States. Here the working class failed altogether to produce a genuinely mass-based movement of its own. This was despite evidence which suggests that, between 1860 and 1913, the economy of the United States was subject to more cycles of boom and bust than the economies of the industrializing countries in Europe. Moreover, the purchasing power of working-class wages rose less rapidly in the United States than in Germany, Great Britain, France, and Sweden — all countries in which important socialist movements were developing at the time.

among the workers can be explained in a number of ways. For one, the United States had a more informal and egalitarian style of life. This more open class structure was partly due to the fact that the United States had no feudal past and its society had not been previously divided into landlords, peasants, and artisans — each with a sharply defined social class-consciousness. Also, the American worker's opportunity to acquire property and to rise from his class, though still small, was considerably greater than that of the proletariat in Europe. This resulted in the average American worker being described at the time as "a sober, calculating businessman without ideals".

But perhaps the most important factor in weakening the ties of common interest and trust so necessary for collective action was that the labouring class in the United States consisted largely of immigrants. They were mostly from a peasant background; only a relatively small number were craftsmen and other skilled workers among whom political radicalism was finding its greatest support. They lived in tightly knit and mutually suspicious ethnic neighbourhoods, and, as a result, national bonds were stronger than class bonds. Also, whenever the United States experienced an economic downturn, many immigrants returned to their native lands, and this is believed to have acted as a political safety-valve.

In sum, by the beginning of the twentieth century, the workers throughout the world had developed a growing sense of identification with existing society. They had come to believe that the capitalist system could give them the better life they aspired to. As the workers displayed a clear preference for security and rewards over struggle and freedom, the labour movement divided sharply between the "social-democratic" and the "communist" versions of Marxism. The latter accused the former of "reformism" (which became later known as "revisionism") — meaning the modification of Marx's revolutionary doctrine. This period was described as the intellectual and political "crisis of Marxism".

In 1914 the German, French, and Belgian Socialist parties voted war credit to enable their bourgeois governments to finance the war. They clearly put patriotism before Marxism. In the *Communist Manifesto* Marx and Engels had called upon the workers of the world to unite, as national interests upon closer examination would always reveal themselves to be no more than the interests of the ruling class. The worker, having no property, had no stake in the country; no one could take away from him what he had not got. Even though internationalism was the very soul and basic principle of socialism, workers' solidarity — which they had expected would abolish wars between nations — was absent.

Marxism in Russia

Marx's analysis was based on conditions in the industrializing countries at the time: Britain, France, and Germany. Nevertheless, Marx was a keen student of Russian affairs and in 1869 even began learning Russian in order to be better able to follow Russian writings and statistics. Marx was convinced that the feudalistic and autocratic regime in Russia was the "bastion of European reaction". Russian troops had suppressed the revolutions in central Europe in 1849, and he strongly believed that they would do it again should a similar situation develop. This shadow Russia was throwing over European revolutionary aspirations moved Marx to attack it again and again to the point of being accused of exhibiting Russophobia. Yet — an "irony of fate", as Marx described it — Russian was the first foreign language into which the first volume of the *Capital* was to be published. In 1872, the censors let it pass because they found it so "difficult and hardly comprehensible" that only "few would read it and still fewer understand it".

Notwithstanding Marx's view of the situation in Russia, Russia had a long tradition of local peasant insurrections, and throughout the nineteenth century a section of the intelligentsia was in revolt against the oppressive autocracy of the Tsar. In the 1870s there was the movement of the *narodniks,* or populists. They were inspired by the work of the First International but believed that Russia should develop a civilization of her own instead of following Western trends. They were oriented towards the peasants instead of the workers of whom there were very few in Russia at the time, and proclaimed that the new social order could be established upon what they perceived as the instinctive preference of the peasant masses for communal ownership of land. They held that a collectivist economic order could be built on the foundation laid by the existing Russian village community, known as *mir*, in which the land was owned in common by the peasants, who were collectively responsible for the payment of taxes and debts.

In the summer of 1874, believing that the revolutionary spirit of the peasants could be harnessed once again and all that was needed was a little prodding to induce them to action, the narodniks organized a "going to the people" pilgrimage. About two thousand students, teachers, and others — an estimated quarter of them women — clad in homespun garments, went to live among the peasants in order to spread the new gospel of a socialist revolution. The *narod* ("people") did not respond to their entreaties and, distrusting all those not of peasant background, often turned them over to the authorities. Having failed to arouse the peasants, a section of the narodniks decided that they would wage a political struggle on behalf of the people. They resorted to isolated acts of terror, arguing that they had to turn to assassinations because, in an authoritarian state, this was the only road to democratic freedom. In 1881 they assassinated Tsar Alexander II.

When the narodniks began resorting to terrorist methods, G.V. Plekhanov — who had been one of the leaders of the narodniks —broke away from the movement, condemning the policy of individual assassination as pointless. In 1879 he fled to Switzerland. There, in collaboration with other exiles, he began to apply the Marxist analysis to Russia and to provide the intellectual leadership for its entire social-democratic movement. In 1881, Vera Zasulich — who was one of the group around Plekhanov — seeking guidance, wrote to Marx. She asked him whether the new order could be built on communal ownership of land without the need of passing through the fires of capitalism as the narodniks believed, or whether the socialists would have to wait the hundreds of years it would take Russia to catch up with the West. At first Marx was evasive: his reply was that his analysis had been based on conditions in the industrial West. However, in the preface to the 1882 Russian edition of the *Communist Manifesto*, he and Engels answered the question with: "If the Russian revolution becomes the signal for the proletarian revolution in the West, so that both complement each other, the Russian common ownership of land may serve as a starting point for communist development."

Towards the end of the nineteenth century a very rapid growth of industry took place mainly around Moscow and Saint Petersburg. For instance, between 1886 and 1899 there was a fivefold rise in iron production. It had been initiated by the Russian government through the banking system and made possible by French, Belgian, German, and British investments and technical and managerial assistance. This upsurge in industrial development was accompanied by a sharp increase in the number of industrial workers who had to labour under the miserable working conditions that characterized the early stage of transition from a basically agrarian to an industrial society.

At the time, apart from the developing revolutionary spirit of the growing number of industrial workers, all over the country there was discontent. There were land-hungry peasants, dissatisfied minor nationalities who represented nearly half of Russia's population, and intellectuals who found the autocratic repression intolerable. Even some members of the middle class and the aristocracy were restless because they felt that there was an overall stagnation in the country. These conditions — particularly since the narodniks had failed to make any headway among the peasants — brought about the replacement of the idea of peasant socialism by that of proletarian socialism. In a number of cities, radical intellectuals organized an active Marxist reform movement. In 1898 a secret conference, attended by fewer than a dozen, proclaimed the foundation of the All-Russian Social Democratic Workers' Party. Nearly all of the participants were shortly after rounded up by the police, but this did not alter the fact that a nationwide workers' party had come into existence.

Vladimir Ilich Ulyanov, better known as Lenin, a lawyer by education, was one of the party's radical leaders. His elder brother had been executed because in 1887 he had taken part in a plot to assassinate Tsar Alexander III. Lenin was a political fighter with a practical organizing ability and an iron will conditioned by Russian revolutionary absolutism. He had embraced Marxism because, as he was to explain, "without a revolutionary theory there can be no revolutionary movement". When the ideas that have sustained a people are failing, they need new ideas to put in their place if they are to agree to a change — and Marx had provided an advanced and ideologically homogeneous scientific theory that proved that there was an alternative to the present order. What is more, basic formulas derived from the Marxist theory provided easy-to-handle and effective answers to the most complex problems.

Lenin stressed the need for an early revolution even though Marx had believed that nothing could or should stop the march of historical evolution. Lenin was unwilling to wait for the dialectic process to unfold. He argued that for a long time to come one could not rely on the Russian bourgeoisie to revolt against the feudal state and introduce the capitalist system. Therefore, it was the proletariat that had to carry out the revolution and put Russia through the industrialization stage. Lenin defended his policy by insisting: "Marxism is not a dogma but a guide to action." While Marx had shown how socialism would be achieved in the Western industrialized countries, he did not proscribe a different approach in other countries. Lenin maintained that as long as the fundamental principles of Marxism were adhered to, modification of form to adapt theory to particular circumstances was excusable.

Lenin did not regard the revolution he was advocating as a socialist revolution. It was to be a "democratic revolution" which would replace the bourgeois one. Instead of ushering in a capitalist order, it would establish a "revolutionary democratic dictatorship of the proletariat and the poor peasantry". It would guide Russia through the industrialization stage and thus, in what Lenin regarded as one continuous process, convert the country from feudalism to communism. And to put this policy into effect, Lenin's immediate objective was to create a small "iron party" — an efficient and dedicated instrument under strong central control — with which to overthrow the Tsarist regime. It had to be an organization that would carry out orders without much questioning, because in conditions of extreme repression as existed in Russia at the time, only a strictly disciplined conspiratorial party could succeed.

Marx saw the small-holding peasants as a vast mass of individuals isolated from one another; they had some intercourse on a local level but lacked a national identity of interests or a political organization and therefore did not form a class. He even compared them with a sack of potatoes. Nevertheless, Lenin, in line with traditional radical thinking in Russia, declared that owing to peculiar circumstances the Russian peasantry were a revolutionary class and the natural allies of the workers. He was fully aware that in order to succeed he needed their support, because at that time Russia's rural population represented 90 per cent of its total population, while the number of industrial workers was still relatively small. The hired agricultural labourers and most of the peasants lived in extreme poverty. Lenin knew that by promising the labourers and the poor peasants the land of the landlords he could enroll them on the side of the revolution. His strategy was: "With all our strength we shall help the peasantry to make the democratic revolution, so that it will be easier for us, the party of the proletariat, to pass over as quickly as possible to the new and higher task of the socialist revolution."

In 1900 Lenin and two young active Marxists called Martov

and Potresov left Russia for Western Europe. Here they obtained the co-operation of Plekhanov, who by now was known as "the grand old man" of Russian Marxism, and of Zasulich and Axelrod, another Russian theoretician living abroad, in the publication of a paper called *Iskra* (the Spark). The paper, printed in very small characters on cigarette paper, was smuggled into Russia and clandestinely distributed by party members in the major industrial centres. By 1902 there was a strong *Iskra* network within Russia spreading the gospel and directing political action. But among the editors themselves, serious dissension was developing. Lenin wanted the agents of *Iskra* to become the nucleus for the strongly organized party of professional revolutionaries he was advocating and thought that the paper should wage an uncompromising struggle against those wavering elements who were obstructing this. He in turn was accused of meaning "the dictatorship over the proletariat" when he spoke about "the dictatorship of the proletariat". This dispute led to an open breach. Lenin resigned from *Iskra* and brought out a paper of his own in which he lambasted his opponents as opportunists and traitors.

At the congress of the All-Russian Social Democratic Workers' Party, held in London in 1903, the party divided into two wings: the Bolsheviks ("majority") and the Mensheviks ("minority"). Although the division did not represent the actual relative strength of the factions, these labels stuck. The Bolsheviks, led by Lenin, accepted his policy of an early revolution engineered by a small party of people who "dedicate to the revolution not a spare evening but the whole of their lives". The Mensheviks, on the other hand, sought to appeal to the masses and wanted to establish a political party similar to those developed in Western Europe. Holding fast to Marx's evolutionary pattern, they contended that Russia, being still a basically agrarian economy, must first pass through the capitalist phase. The workers could not fulfil a role for which they were not ready. The Mensheviks wanted to co-operate with the liberal middle-class parties with the purpose of moving them to revolutionary action that would establish a capitalist soceity. And, while capitalism was to carry out its task of industrializing Russia, they would assume the role of an ordinary socialist opposition in a parliamentary capitalist republic, guard the interests of the working class and prepare them for the socialist revolution.

Lenin described as "economism" this trend designed to allow the whole labour movement to concentrate its energies on furthering economic goals such as higher wages, shorter hours, and better working conditions while the middle-class liberals established capitalism. He quoted Marx's dictum that "if a workers' movement is not revolutionary, it is nothing" and declared that the first task of trade unions was to develop the political consciousness of the workers. To him economism was nothing but an opportunism of the type that amounted to heresy. Workers were being led astray. Economism provided the basis for "class peace" and the development of a reformist consciousness and thus deflected the proletariat from promoting its historic real interests — that is, to liberate itself by abolishing all private property. In 1912 the great divergence in approach led the Bolsheviks and the Mensheviks to split formally into separate parties.

In the meantime, an industrial depression and the humiliating defeat of Russia by Japan had acted as a catalyst to spontaneous unrest and riots. Although largely inspired by the narodniks (who in 1901 had reorganized themselves as the Social Revolutionary Party), the revolutionary activity lacked any specific direction. It all started in Saint Petersburg, in January 1905, with a peaceful demonstration by many thousands of unarmed workers who, accompanied by their wives and children, marched to present a petition to the Tsar. The demonstrators were fired on by the police; more than seventy died, and many hundreds were wounded. The incident became known as the massacre of "bloddy Sunday". This was followed by a wave of strikes, demonstrations, assassination of officials, peasants pillaging and breaking into the mansions of the nobility, and the mutiny on the battleship *Potemkin*. Liberal, radical, and other groups were demanding parliamentary government and the institution of universal suffrage. In Saint Petersburg the Soviet (Council) of Workers' Deputies was formed; although it was conceived merely as a central strike committee, its leadership perceived that it could be turned into an organ for political agitation and revolution. All this activity culminated in October in a general strike.

In 1906 Russia settled down. The Tsar had announced the creation of a parliament called the Imperial Duma, and although executive authority remained in the hands of the Tsar and his ministers, who were not responsible to the Duma, liberal discontent was appeased, particularly because the sabre-rattling of the Soviet of Workers' Deputies had discouraged the middle class from further political activism. The peasants' temper was soothed when, in 1907, the Tsar gave them the right to have their land in a single consolidated holding.

But the events of 1905 had some fundamental effects. One was the realization that in Russia the masses could be stirred into action. Until then the struggle against the Tsarist autocracy had been predominantly an affair of individuals and small circles which were eventually betrayed by a spy or a traitor and broken up by wholesale arrests by the police. Another major effect was that workers could exercise the right to organize trade unions and mutual-aid societies — as long as they abstained from politics. Yet perhaps the most important effect was that the number of the landless peasantry increased. This was a corollary of efficient farmers accumulating large holdings as a result of the new land policies. Thus a huge reservoir of discontent was created that could be easily exploited.

Lenin, who had returned to Russia in 1905, left once again in 1907 because he believed that he could lead the movement better from abroad than from a hiding place inside the country. In the years that followed, by his literary work he carried out the crucial task of extending Marx's theory and gave it an appearance of continued relevance despite changing circumstances that were not in accord with Marx's expectations. For instance, the emergence of limited liability companies had resulted in many people who could not be classed as wealthy and powerful acquiring shares in companies and thus becoming co-owners of the means of production. Lenin (broadly in line with a conclusion Marx had also reached) overcame this by asserting that capitalism had ceased to function in the "normal" way — the free market competition was being replaced by capitalist monopolies which were regimenting and dominating the system. Banks had also developed from modest intermediary enterprises into a few monopolies. Their capital, merged with that of the industrial monopolists, Lenin called "finance capital". Having the control over this finance capital had enabled bankers and some other financial groups to exert an overriding influence within the system. The state had become their servant. Thus the finance capitalists, or financiers, were representing the real power within the capitalist system. This new oligarchy had assumed the position previously held by the industrial capitalists.

The growing prosperity of the capitalist economies and the failure of the wage workers to become pauperized and perform the act of the proletarian revolution, Lenin explained, was the result of "imperialism". His book *Imperialism, the Highest Stage of Capitalism*, written in 1916, is regarded by many Marxists as a direct continuation of *Capital*, as it elaborates on Marx's theme of the advent of imperialism dominated by the economic competition between advanced countries. The central thesis of Lenin's analysis is that the finance capitalists were being driven outwards in their search for profitable outlets for the mounting accumulation of capital, and this was leading to the spread of international capitalist monopolies. During this imperialist phase — which Lenin described as a special stage of development of capitalism — Western capitalist countries were acquiring colonies to enable their monopolies to use them as a source of cheap raw materials and a dumping ground for the commodities they could not sell at home. This accounted for the fact that there was no slackening in the accumulation of capital assets. Moreover, the capitalists were in the position to make "super profits" which enabled them to pay higher wages to the workers and to bribe and corrupt their leaders. As a result, for a time, a "considerable minority" of the working class renounced its revolutionary role. In short, by exploiting the toiling masses in the backward countries and because of "the extraordinary rapidity and particularly revolting character of the development of opportunism" in the whole labour movement, the capitalists had not only avoided economic and political disaster at home but also maintained a certain degree of prosperity.

But all this had achieved was to shift the class struggle into the international arena. It could not prolong the existence of capitalism much longer. Imperialism was the final stage: capitalism had reached its unsurpassable limits. Because the partition of all the territory of the earth by the greatest capitalist countries had been completed, the fight between competing large national trusts for colonial raw materials and markets had brought in its wake national rivalries. In the scramble to survive, capitalist countries were seizing upon each other, and this was giving the proletariat the opportunity to make their revolution. And production and distribution having become to a great extent international in their operation, the whole world was drawn into the capitalist system. This meant that capitalism could be attacked in any part of the globe. Thus Lenin, through his finance capital and imperialist theories, provided a theoretical justificaiton for a revolution in such industrially backward countries as Russia.

Lenin was in Switzerland during the 1914-18 war. He declared that this "imperialist war" must be turned into a civil one; this war of nations must become a resolute conflict between the proletariat and the ruling classes. Russia had entered the war because she too was in the race for markets; owing to the poverty of her people she could not consume all the goods she produced. He proclaimed that the great honour of initiating a wave of socialist revolutions, which would arise with "objective inevitability" from the war, had fallen to the Russian proletariat. However, he did not believe that the honour of being the vanguard of revolutionary action in Europe was theirs because Russia had an inherent superiority — on the contrary, it was because she was "the weakest link in the capitalist chain".

In the meantime, in Russia, after huge losses on the battlefield, the army felt betrayed and wasted. In the country there was a profound disgust for the Tsar and his regime. Transport services had broken down, and food and fuel supplies were completely disorganized. A series of demonstrations, which the government was powerless to stop, led to the Tsar's abdication in February 1917. A "provisional government" was formed which included aristocrats, liberals, social revolutionaries, and (although not at first) Mensheviks. They were mainly uninspiring individuals who disagreed among themselves. Meanwhile, all over the country, soviets of delegates of workers, peasants, and soldiers were set up. They had a great hold on the people, and as they gave only qualified support to the authorities, the provisional government was weak to the point of impotence. Because the provisional government could not rely on the support of the police or the army, especially in the event of a clash with the soviets, the soviets became the centres of real power. At first the town soviets were dominated by the Mensheviks and the village soviets by the social revolutionaries, but gradually they came more and more under Bolshevik influence.

As the provisional government did not seek peace, the Germans — recognizing Lenin's potential to disrupt the Russian war effort — allowed him to travel across Germany to Sweden whence he returned home. When he arrived in Petrograd on 16 April he was welcomed by crowds of workers, sailors, soldiers, and representatives of various revolutionary organizations carrying red banners. Lenin perceived his opportunity. With the gospel of class war and promises of land to the peasants, control of production to the workers, and peace to the soldiers, he provided brilliant revolutionary leadership. Peasants began seizing the land of the landlords, and workers began taking over the factories, while soldiers mutinied. Because in each army unit its soviet had to countersign every order issued by officers before it was obeyed, there was no military discipline and the troops rapidly turned into a mass of armed peasants eager to return home and share in the spoils. While the army disintegrated and the front collapsed, the national economic life became chaotic. The little control of the country retained by the provisional government slipped out of its hands. In November 1917, after an almost bloodless coup, the Bolsheviks captured power first in Petrograd and then in Moscow. Thus the first state flying the Marxist banner came into being. But, instead of establishing a "revolutionary democratic dictatorship of the proletariat and the poor peasantry", Lenin proclaimed the "dictatorship of the proletariat".

As noted earlier, Lenin perceived the revolution in Russia

only as the advance guard of the world proletarian revolution, which he declared as "never so close at hand as now". Therefore, the immediate task was merely to retain soviet power. The Bolsheviks (who soon after were to rename themselves the Communist Party) issued two decrees the next day after their victory. One of the decrees ordered the nationalization of the banking institutions; the other expropriated all the large estates, which were to be handed over to local agrarian committees. The first was to ensure them the finances they needed, the second to gain the support of the peasantry.

Because Lenin believed that the workers of the other nations involved in the war would also carry out a revolution and that there would be "peace over the heads of governments between the peoples who are overthrowing them", the soldiers on the front were instructed to fraternize with enemy soldiers. But Lenin's expectations failed to eventuate, and after some delaying tactics he was forced to accept very harsh peace terms, as he felt not to do so would imperil soviet power.

In order to put into effect the "dictatorship of the proletariat", there was a need for strong internal policies and — because, according to Lenin, all means that lead towards the goal are justified — the suppression of all civil liberties. Gradually all opposition newspapers were closed down and a secret, all-powerful political police was created. It was an instrument for organized, systematic mass terror with a network of agents that extended throughout the whole of Russia. Its unbridled terror was such as the world had never seen before. People were executed on the slightest suspicion or as hostages; prisons and concentration camps filled.

The humiliating peace treaty, the loss of all civil liberties, the terror, and the generally chaotic economic situation within Russia led to increasing revolt from every level of the Russian people. The new government was forced to fight, for two years, a bitter and ferocious civil war. Leon Trotsky, a Marxist journalist who had pursued an independent course between the Bolsheviks and the Mensheviks but had joined Lenin during the revolution, founded and organized a new regular army. It replaced the amateur Red Guards who were little more than groups of armed factory workers. The Red Army, as it was called, had to fight not only the Russian "White Army" but also British, French, Japanese, and United States troops who intervened primarily with the purpose of preventing Russian war supplies from being handed over to the Germans. There is little doubt that the French and British were also keen to save their huge investments in Russia. The civil war caused great devastation, hunger, and chaos. After defeating its enemies, the "revolution" eliminated all "counter-revolutionaries" — these included the Mensheviks and the social revolutionaries who, until then, had been able to survive despite harassment.

The Bolsheviks accused the Western Socialist parties of having betrayed the principles of the Second International by supporting the war efforts of their respective bourgeois governments. They described them as traitors and the "lackeys of capitalism". In March 1919 they founded the Communist International (the Third International), which came to be known as the Comintern. Lenin used the term *Communist* in order to repudiate all connection with the Socialist, or Second, International and the European Socialist parties, and to proclaim its affinity with the original Communist League.

Lenin (and Trotsky) attached great importance to the Comintern. Lenin was determined to forge the Communist parties of the world into tightly organized and genuinely militant bodies similar to the pattern he had devised for the Russian party. The Comintern was to have one clear aim, which was to organize world revolution. Because of the numerical weakness of the proletariat in Russia and the conservatism of a peasantry that was more concerned with an extra acre of land than with socialism, Lenin was convinced that the success of his revolution still depended upon the support of the proletariat in the Western European countries. There was no guarantee against counter-revolution in Russia without victorious revolutions in a number of other countries.

The Comintern, which was to be helped and advised by its sponsor, the Russian party, came under its influence from the beginning. The Russian party enjoyed the esteem derived from being the architect of the first successful socialist revolution. But it was also the Comintern's major financial contributor, and a number of European parties, which had only relatively small following of their own, depended largely on funds from the Comitern. Rigid conditions were imposed on all that joined, and those that did not unconditionally support Moscow's interpretation of Marxism and its application to the realities around them were expelled.

Communist parties were instructed to strive incessantly for power. In order to achieve it, they had to learn "how to combine the strictest loyalty to the ideas of communism and the ability to make all necessary compromises — to tack, make agreements, zig-zags, retreats, and so on". They were to impose the strongest discipline on all their members, who had to be "true Communists". A true Communist was defined as one who is completely "party minded" — that is, he unquestioningly serves the party's objectives; he fully accepts the Communist ideology and is so convinced that he works with history's blessing that he never concedes that the opposition has a point. He is a distinct type of human being: austere and resolute. In short, he is a dedicated professional revolutionary.

The Communists were to work through governments, trade unions, front organizations, and the like. Whatever means they used were morally justifiable. In the struggle for absolute justice, the end justified the means. Lenin's dictum was: "We do not believe in an eternal morality", and "We say: morality is what serves to destroy the old exploiting society and to unite all the toilers around the proletariat, which is creating a new society." The entire fabric of the capitalist societies had to be turned upside down and rebuilt on a wholly new foundation. Then, and only then, through service and social action could the world order foreseen by Marx be established. In other words, morality simply meant doing what had to be done to make a socialist revolution. Social movements were not good or bad but "progressive" when they assisted the historical process perceived by Marx and "reactionary" when they frustrated it. The class struggle was an unending battle in which no quarter should be given and none should be expected from the other side. As the world was divided into two camps, there was no room for an intermediate position. Nothing mattered except the absolute victory of the proletariat. In 1920 Lenin wrote: "As long as capitalism and socialism remain side by side we cannot live peacefully — the one or the other will be victor in the end."

In the industrialized countries, Communist parties were instructed to take advantage of any national, ethnic, or racial conflict. They were to foment existing grievances and, if there were none, create them. They were not to view right-wing parties as their immediate enemies because they could deal with them at leisure after the revolution. The real enemy was the Socialist parties, because they competed on the same ground — they were working towards obtaining the goodwill of the workers.*

Work within the trade unions was to be one of the most important tasks of the Communists. They were to exploit every crisis that could lead to a strike. This approach was in sharp contrast to that accepted by the Socialist trade union leaders who — being aware of the suffering a strike can cause the workers and their families — called a strike only when they believed that the complaint was genuine and it lay within the powers of the industry to remedy the situation. To the Communists, the purpose of a strike was not to improve the lot of the workers but to create a situation in which the question of private property and exploitation could be brought to the front and the political awareness of the workers developed. This would bring about an ever-expanding union of the workers and lead to class-conflict and eventually to revolution. In sum, the narrow economic struggles of the working class had to be transformed into broad political ones. To achieve this, according to Lenin, a Communist had to "be prepared to make every sacrifice and, if necessary, even resort to all sorts of schemes and stratagems, employ illegal methods, conceal the truth, in order to get into the trade unions, stay there, and conduct the revolutionary work within".

And because Lenin believed that capitalist countries would perish more quickly if deprived of their colonial domains,

---

* Later, in Germany, as a result of this policy, the Socialists and the Communists did not enter into an arrangement to establish some sort of working-class unity and combine to prevent the acquisition of power by Hitler, who, once in power, destroyed them both.

"anti-imperialism" was adopted as one of the major weapons in the arsenal of the Comintern. To cut off this source of capitalist prosperity, people living in the colonies of foreign powers and semi-colonial countries such as China were to be indoctrinated into regarding themselves as the victims of imperialism, and the local Communist parties were to support all national liberation movements, including those led by the bourgeoisie.

Now let us return to developments within Russia. The civil war, as already mentioned, caused widespread destitution. The situation was aggravated by the reckless requisitioning of all surplus products from the peasants who then had no incentive to produce anything more than they themselves could consume, and by the large-scale nationalization of industry carried out by people who were not equipped for this kind of task. Private trade in consumer goods was prohibited, the state conducted moneyless transactions with non-state enterprises, and wages were paid in kind, as paper money had virtually lost all value. Problems piled up, and in 1921 Russia was on the verge of complete economic collapse. This led to a number of disturbances, localized peasant revolts, industrial strikes, and the mutiny of the sailors at the important naval base at Kronstadt.

Lenin, by nature a realist, became impatient whenever dogma looked like obstructing the practical approach. Besides, not only had Marx never formulated a clear-cut model for building the kind of society he envisaged but also Lenin had to build socialism in conditions radically different from those Marx expected to exist. In order to save Russia from political chaos, Lenin introduced what he called the New Economic Policy. He described the preceding three terrible years as "war communism" and blamed them on the abnormal conditions of war and civil war. His New Economic Policy tolerated some small-scale private enterprise and sanctioned overtime and piece-work payments to workers in factories. Control of administration and industry by committee was scrapped; business managers began operating under state licence. The requisitioning of all surplus farm produce stopped; peasants were now required to surrender only one-tenth of their total output and allowed to sell their surplus in the open market at market prices. Money reappeared as the prime means of exchange.

Lenin justified his retreat from full socialism by confessing: "We went too far on the path of nationalization of commerce and industry and the suppression of local trade", and stated that it was "not the growth of the petty bourgeoisie and the small capitalist" that had to be feared, but "the prolongation of famine, of misery, of shortage of food". He stressed that "equality is an empty phrase unless by equality is meant the abolition of classes" but admitted that the transition to communism would be impossible to achieve without using the technical and managerial expertise of people from the bourgeois class.

In other words, the time had come when a philosophy of revolution had to be converted into a philosophy of government. Lenin was now a ruler who had to compromise with the theory. But by formulating strategy in Marxist terms and using Marxist rhetoric, he managed to give the impression that Marx continued to be relevant. His interpretations of the theory were accepted because by this time he was seen as the one who embodied the "unity of theory and practice" that was so important to Marx, and thus was the fund of all Communist wisdom. What later came to be known as Marxism-Leninism began to enjoy full ideological monopoly.

In 1922 the Union of Soviet Socialist Republics was proclaimed. Workers, peasants, and soldiers were given voting rights; all the other elements of society were excluded from political power. The USSR was to be a proletarian democracy consisting of soviets of workers and peasants operating on many levels of a pyramidal structure within each republic. According to the statutes, the soviets were to send delegates to the Congress of the Soviet Union, which represented the supreme authority. It elected the Central Committee to act on behalf of the Congress when it was not in session and to elect the members of the Politburo and other central organs. To this day the soviets, which are guided by the Communist Party, are the nominal rulers of the country.

But Lenin did not see the Soviet Union as being on the threshold of socialism, because the "transformation of the peasant's psychology and habits is something that requires generations". And as he had ceased to believe that the people were capable of regulating their political, economic, and intellectual life, he returned to his pre-revolutionary concept of a strong and centrally controlled party. All non-Communists were expelled from the soviets, which as a consequence lost their character of freely elected bodies. The USSR, despite its name, was not to become a decentralized democracy, and Marx's concept of a dictatorship of the overwhelming majority over an isolated capitalist bourgeoisie was translated into a dictatorship of the Communist minority over the vast majority of the people. The dictatorship of the proletariat gave way to the dictatorship of the party. But, within the party, there was still what was called "democratic centralism". On many issues party members, individually and even in groups, could voice opinions, but once a decision was reached at the top, any further public disagreement was condemned as "fractionalism" and dealt with as treason.

Party members were described as the vanguard of the proletariat. Lenin argued that, by having been chosen from the most highly developed section of the working class and by keeping in touch with the workers, party members expressed what the more backward elements would desire were they sufficiently mature to discern where their true interests lay. In other words, the masses were being guided in a regimented fashion towards participation in the creation of a new order. The authoritarian environment that existed under the Tsar was being perpetuated by Lenin. This was made possible by the age-old apathy of the Russian people, who had learned to resign themselves to the idea that state power was the preserve of a privileged group.

In 1924 Lenin died, and the leadership of the Soviet Union transferred to triumvirate of which Joseph Stalin was a member. Unlike Lenin and Trotsky, Stalin was not a good orator or agitator and during the events of 1917 had not played a conspicuous role, although he was active as the editor of the party newspaper *Pravda*. In 1922 Stalin had been appointed secretary-general of the party and — being ultimately responsible for all appointments, promotions, demotions, and transfers of its members — soon came to control its whole machinery. As a result, he was the most powerful member of the triumvirate.

Within the party, Trotsky was the centre of a "leftish" opposition to Stalin. There had always been personal rivalry and ideological and political conflict between the two. Trotsky persisted in his belief that the ultimate triumph of socialism within the Soviet Union would become possible only after the victory of the proletariat in the most industrialized countries in Europe. Since Russia was a backward peasant country, if no help would be forthcoming from these countries, productivity and the standard of living would continue to remain lower than in the capitalist countries, with the result that socialism in the Soviet Union would eventually collapse. Already in 1906, Trotsky had formulated a doctrine of "permanent revolution". The idea had its origin in Marx's "Address to the Central Committee of the Communist League" in 1850 in which he declared that it would be in the interest of, and therefore the task of, the League to "make revolution permanent, until all more or less possessing classes have been forced out of their position of dominance" and in all dominant countries of the world "at least the decisive productive forces are concentrated in the hands of the proletariat". Trotsky argued that because capitalism had entered the imperialist stage there was a world interrelation between production and distribution, and this made it impossible to deal with capitalism within the confines of only one country. The confrontation between the capitalists and the working classes being international, one could not cut off revolution at any one point. It had to be an uninterrupted process: as soon as the revolution was successful in one country, as in the case of Russia, steps had to be taken to extend it to another until all class society was liquidated.

Stalin, on the other hand, advocated a policy of "socialism in one country". Unlike Lenin, Trotsky, and other Bolshevik leaders, Stalin had never lived as an exile in Europe and never fully shared their confidence that there was a revolutionary movement in Western Europe. Being a "home-bred" Bolshevik, he was always predisposed towards the traditional

Russian belief in national self-sufficiency. After the crushing of the Bulgarian insurrection and the retreat from revolution by the German Workers' Party in 1923, and the collapse of the Estonian attempt at insurrection in 1924, Stalin could forcefully argue that because Europe had "temporarily stabilized", the time had come for the Soviet Union to build up its own strength so that its survival should not depend upon a world revolution.

In 1925, to the relief of the Russian people and the world at large, the party accepted Stalin's policy. From the Russian people — who, in any case, were always uncomfortable with the revolutionary internationalism of the Lenin era — it removed the fear of having to go through another civil war if other countries did not establish socialism. It also reduced world tension and hostility — but did not bring about a more friendly collaboration between the Soviet Union and other countries.

Within the country, Stalin began introducing tighter controls. He abolished whatever freedom of expression existed within the Communist party itself. This resulted in further clashes with Trotsky, who wanted the Soviet Union to become a true proletarian democracy — meaning by this an "open" party that allowed for varying political tendencies and enabled the younger generation to have a greater influence on decision-making. Also, Trotsky had argued that the true ends of communism could not be attained by employing the concept that every and any type of action was permissible in certain circumstances. While Trotsky did not oppose coercion as such — in fact he had employed terror tactics himself — he believed that it should be possible to strike a balance between dictatorship and freedom, the latter gaining a larger and larger share as the system achieved stability. In 1927 Stalin managed to have Trotsky expelled from the party and, because at the time Stalin still accepted the rule that a Communist should never be put to death for merely political opposition to the current party leadership, banished to Central Asia. In 1929 Trotsky was sent into exile.

Stalin also strengthened the already powerful oppressive apparatus. He reasoned that the state needed more power before

it withered away, because the bourgeoisie was not fully eliminated. This was partly true because Lenin's economic policy
had enabled some farmers and middlemen to become better
off. Thus Stalin was in a position to build a theoretical bridge
between the Marxist doctrine and his activities.

Gradually, Stalin established himself as the undisputed
ruler of the Soviet Union. The dictatorship of the party was
replaced by a personal dictatorship. The party was converted
into a highly centralized and disciplined bureaucracy. The
most perfect totalitarian order came into being. No sphere of
individual life was allowed to escape its all-embracing reach.
The security police had at its absolute mercy all but the party
members, who, however, were under the direct control of the
local party branches. There was no redress against any arbitrary
action.

Lenin's New Economic Policy was brought to an end and
replaced by a series of five-year plans. Their purpose was to accelerate the pace of industrialization. Stalin declared: "We are
fifty or a hundred years behind the advanced countries. We
must make up this lag in ten years. Either we do it, or they
crush us." Stalin became an industrialization despot who ruled
over a terribly brutal period that was to drag Russia, a huge and
wild country, into the twentieth century. All considerations for
human life, liberty, and individual rights were brushed aside.

To begin with, in order to free labour for industry while at
the same time keeping up production of food to feed a swelling
urban population, Stalin set out to reorganize agriculture.
Between 1929 and 1933 more than a hundred million peasants
were compelled to give up their primitive small holdings,
which were amalgamated into collective farms in which machinery and large-scale methods of cultivation were used. At
first, collectivization was a failure and led to widespread
famine. Peasants were not only deprived of their land but,
because of the high priority given to heavy industry, they were
also unable to obtain the consumer goods they were ac-
customed to. They showed their bitter discontent by slaughter-
ing half of their livestock to sell or eat, smashing their imple-
ments and burning their crops, instead of handing them over
to collective ownership. This brought on ruthless oppression:

thousands were killed and hundreds of thousands were up-rooted and dumped on the outskirts of developing industrial towns or placed in one of many huge labour camps and compelled to build roads, railways, and canals, to fell timber, and the like.

In order to encourage skill and efficiency, Stalin fought the egalitarian trends among some party members to whom he referred as "the levellers". He declared that equality was "alien and detrimental to socialist production", and that the Soviet Union was still a dictatorship of the proletariat; in this transitional stage, equality merely meant that no class should exploit another. People could still be paid according to their ability and work, and not according to their needs. This line of reasoning provided him with the theoretical justification for allowing the newly created collectives to develop into co-operatives instead of developing into communes. Members — besides being allowed to own small plots of land, poultry, and some cattle — shared in the collective's profits. This enabled the members of one collective to be better off than those of another. In the industrial field, Stalin enforced incentive rewards to the skilled workers, technicians, and administrators. The media extolled the virtues of the "heroes of the productive front".

In 1933 Hitler came to power in Germany. He had declared that he would destroy communism. Stalin was convinced that Germany, with the encouragement and connivance of the Western capitalist countries, would attack the Soviet Union. This brought about changes in policy. Internally he extended the concept of "socialism in one country" to "nationalistic communism". Russian traditions and patrotism were revived — notwithstanding Marx's idea that workers owed loyalty to no particular country. Abroad, Communist parties were instructed to join "anti-Fascist" movements instead of holding aloof from other parties of the Left. After 1935 the defence of democracy (including bourgeois democracy) against fascism became the supreme task of the Comintern.

In 1936 a new constitution proclaimed the victory of socialism — but not the advent of communism — within the Soviet Union. It announced that the bourgeois class was eliminated and as a result there was no further need for a dictatorship of the proletariat. Despite the new constitution, nothing changed. Stalin continued to rule and remained a dictator with unlimited powers. The state was not destined to disappear. Stalin's explanation was that the state could fade away only when the Soviet Union was surrounded by other Socialist states, and not while it was still encircled by hostile capitalist countries and in danger of a foreign military attack. The state must not only survive but be made stronger. However, Stalin pointed out that under socialism the state was the servant not of a particular section of society but of society as a whole. In other words, in the Soviet Union, the transition from socialism to communism would have to await the international revolution.

Between 1936 and 1938 there took place what became known as the Great Purges. Almost everyone who had manifested critical and independent thought, or who in any other way represented a real or imagined threat to Stalin and his policies, was eliminated. Among the victims were nearly the whole of the old guard of Bolsheviks (including Kamenev and Zinoviev, who were the other two members of the triumvirate that governed the Soviet Union immediately after Lenin's death), 98 of the 139 members and candidates of the Central Committee of the party, and more than half of the army commanders. Thousands more were executed, tens of thousands imprisoned, and hundreds of thousands sent into concentration camps. Those who were brought to public trial were charged with attempting to assassinate Stalin or some other leader, or to restore capitalism, or to destroy the country's economy or its military power, or with carrying out espionage on behalf of a foreign power regarded as hostile to the Soviet Union. Before their trials they were subjected to physical and mental torture. In addition, in accordance with a decree authorized by Stalin in 1934 that proclaimed the collective responsibility of every family for treason committed by one of its members, relatives were used as hostages. During the trials, defendants "confessed" and indulged in self-criticism and self-condemnation, without any internationally accepted legal evidence being produced against them. Their behaviour may be explained partly by the fact that many of them felt a basic loyalty towards the social order that had become identified with Stalin's rule. Others may have expected to save their lives. Very few did.

In the late 1930s, it seemed likely that Stalin would enter into arrangements with Britain and France to contain Hitler. However, the Western leaders proved somewhat lukewarm during the negotiations. After the Communist involvement in semi-revolutionary occupation of factories in France in 1936, and the revolutionary regime created by armed workers in Madrid and Barcelona in the same year, many Westerners had come to regard communism as a greater threat than fascism. Britain and France tried a policy of appeasement of Germany. Stalin, who had no real preference for bourgeois democracies as against fascism, netotiated openly with the Western democracies and secretly with Hitler. In August 1939, after the Germans offered the partition of Eastern Europe between Germany and the Soviet Union, Stalin signed a Russian-German friendship and non-aggression pact, notwithstanding his earlier maxim: "We want not a single foot of anybody's land." It seemed to be a shrewd tactical move to extend the border of the Soviet Union while at the same time keeping aloof from what he described as the "new imperialist war". But the pact did not stop Germany from attacking the Soviet Union in 1941 without provocation. Thus Russia became an ally of the Western powers.

During the war the Comintern, which had not been successful in bringing about a single Communist revolution in Western Europe and had not held a congress since 1935, was formally dissolved. Ever since its formation the Comintern had been a heavy liability for the Soviet Union's foreign policy and greatly contributed to the country's pre-war isolation. Stalin felt that its continued existence would only embarrass the Allied war effort. Its dissolution was to confirm abroad his policy of "socialism in one country" and thus make post-war peaceful co-existence seem a real possibility. It was to act as a proof that in the future it would be possible to deal with the Soviet Union as with any other nation state — that is, as with any other country that is primarily concerned with its own interests and is not involved in promoting revolution abroad.

However, this was not to be the case. When the war was over, the Soviet Union returned to its old policies based upon the idea that the world was divided into two camps: the capitalist and the Communist. The alliances entered into during the war were discarded as tactical moves. Stalin had pledged to respect the rights of the people in the countries in Eastern Europe "liberated" by the Red Army to choose their own form of government. Despite this pledge, by the beginning of 1949 all effective opposition to the Communists was eliminated. These countries had been converted into Communist-ruled satellites, totally dependent upon the Soviet Union economically as well as militarily. The Communist takeovers were carried out in three distinct stages. First, to accord with the agreements reached between the Allies, the Communists participated in a genuine left-wing coalition in which the non-Communist element accepted Communist leadership. Together they eliminated all right-wing political leaders. Second, the Communists rendered the coalition unworkable and dispatched the Socialist leaders one by one as they had served their purpose. Third, when the machinery of government was completely in their hands, they proclaimed the state a "people's democracy" which performs the function of a dictatorship of the proletariat that, guided by the Soviet Union, builds socialism.

In 1947 an organization called the Communist Information Agency, or Cominform for short, was set up. Through it the Russian party spoke and, despite the dissolution of the Comintern, Communist parties all over the world listened and tried to follow the line laid down by Moscow. It declared that "the Communists must close their ranks, unite their efforts on the basis of the common anti-imperialist and democratic platform, and rally aound them all the democratic and patriotic forces of the people". Loyalty to communism still implied loyalty to the Soviet Union, and until the mid-1950s "socialism in one country" was replaced by "socialism in one camp".

But Stalin was not free of all opposition from within Communist ranks. Before the war, some highly articulate Communist intellectuals had rallied around Trotsky. In 1938 they set up what they somewhat optimistically called the Fourth

International. Apart from a proletarian world revolution, they wanted a political revolution within the Soviet Union. It would overthrow the party machinery and administrative bureaucracy and install a real proletarian democracy — that is, rule by the soviets. They intended to abolish ranks and decorations and all other kinds of privileges and to distribute the national income in accordance with what Trotsky had described as "the interest and will of the worker and peasant masses". In 1940 Trotsky was assassinated, and his followers had to carry on without his guidance. Although the Fourth International split in 1953, Trotskyist groupings continued to be active and important — especially in South America and in some developing countries.

Also, the Yugoslav party, the only East European Communist party that had come to power mainly through its own efforts (as a result of having provided the leadership of wartime resistance to the German occupation of the country), refused to follow the Stalinist line. It "deviated" in the direction of European liberalism and permissiveness towards human individualism. It argued that the Communist movement should take account of the changing conditions within the economically advanced countries of Western Europe. There was no need either for a revolution, as the working class could assume power through the democratic process, or to pass through the stage of the dictatorship of the proletariat, because capitalism was decaying into "state capitalism". Tito, the leader of the Yugoslav party, was denounced as Fascist, and the country was subjected to an economic and military blockade by the Soviet bloc. When Yugoslavia accepted economic aid from the United States, Tito was described not only as a tool and willing puppet of imperialism but also as the worst enemy of the working class. A number of East European leaders, who also attempted to assert their self-respect and find a "national road to socialism", were branded as traitors in collusion with Titoism or Trotskyism, imprisoned, made to "confess" their sins at trials modelled on those of the Great Purges in Moscow, and executed.

In the Western countries, public opinion — which during the war years was subjected to pro-Soviet indoctrination —

took some time to adjust itself to the new political reality. But the extension of Soviet power into Eastern Europe, and the growing Communist influence in the rest of the world, revived the dormant anit-Communist sentiments in the United States and in much of Europe. The idea that the Soviet Union had to be contained came to be accepted. This resulted in mounting tension and intensive rearmament in both the Western and the Communist worlds and grew into what came to be known as the cold war.

Stalin died in 1953. His achievements were demonstrably great and, being the "father of victory" in the desperately fought war that could not have been won without the large-scale collectivization and intense industrialization he had forced upon the Russian people, he was the subject of a great deal of adulation at the time of his death. But by this time he was already an anachronism in the modernized Russia of his own making, for which the people of the Soviet Union had had to pay such a tragically high price. He had replaced Marx's humanitarian and internationalist aims by suppression, nationalism, and military expansionism. Stalin had perfected the highly centralized and all-powerful state he inherited from Lenin in which propaganda went hand in hand with police surveillance and terror. Private property disappeared, but the means of production and distribution, instead of passing to the people to be managed from below by the immediate producers in direct association, were managed by the vast bureaucratic machine. In other words, industry was nationalized instead of being socialized. As a result, the Soviet Union has now a totalitarian state economy and not a society in which men cooperate freely because of the community's mastery over the process of production. Within the framework of a welfare state, the Soviet Union is a dictatorship not of, but over, the proletariat and the peasantry. A small clique at the top has the full monopoly of power and a well-organized party to implement it. The Soviet Union has little in common with Marx's broad vision of the future socialist society. It is an autocratic system wearing a Marxist mask.

Nevertheless, one cannot dismiss Stalinism — as many would like to — as a moral and political corruption of

Marxism. Despite all the terrible things perpetrated in the name of Marxism-Leninism, Stalinism is important in the history of communism. For twenty-five years, from 1928 to 1953, it dominated Communist practices and theories. During this time, Russia — a backward peasant country isolated and threatened by enemies outside and within — was industrialized in an amazingly short time. Stalin created the economic base — which Marx believed would take a whole capitalist epoch to build — which was the prerequisite upon which a communist society could be erected. What is more, he proved to the world that communism was a political system that could relatively quickly transform a backward society into a modern one without dependence on foreign capital.

Stalin's successors broke away from Stalinist orthodoxy and embarked on what they called a "new course". The party re-emerged as the apparent prime agency of rule. Also the oligarchic character of the party was restored when one-man leadership was replaced by a kind of collective leadership. There is now a less totalitarian approach and the security police appear to have lost some of their powers. In general, there is more respect for the rule of the law, a relaxation of censorship, and liberalization in cultural life.

Policy towards the outside world became less militant after Stalin. One reason for it was that during the 1950s the hydrogen bomb was developed. This, plus the advent of long-range ballistic missiles and nuclear submarines, raised the level of the "balance of terror". In 1956 Nikita Khrushchev, at the time the leader in the Soviet Union, declared that war was no longer "fatally inevitable" and that neither side would escape utter destruction in an all-out nuclear war. Because of this stalemate, the traditional ideas of victory and defeat in war were no longer applicable. But, Khrushchev said, the political struggle would continue and the victory of communism would be achieved "in peaceful competition with capitalism". He must have come to the conclusion that, owing to the economic strength of Western society, the main task of the Soviet Union was to catch up and outstrip the most developed capitalist countries in production per capita. He relied on the inherently superior capacity of a planned economy to expand production.

Once the standard of living in Communist countries overtook that in the Western countries, the masses of the world would be attracted irresistibly towards communism.

Propaganda was accepted as the most apropriate form of intensifying the class war in non-Communist countries. Soviet-inspired "peace movements" were set up around the world which initiated "anti-imperialist" campaigns. They branded all those who proved to be an obstacle to Communist ambitions as warmongers. The promotion of cultural exchanges with Western countries was another feature of the Soviet propaganda campaign. The Soviet leaders, in line with Marxist-Leninist expectations, must have hoped that the relaxation of the Stalinist confrontation would not only reinforce internal class conflicts but also rekindle the "imperialist conflict" among the capitalist nations.

Apart from the nuclear stalemate, there was another very important reason that contributed to the decline in soviet militancy. The spread of communism, as the aftermath of the war, had brought about a completely new situation. After Stalin's death, the "indestructible" Communist monolith gradually began losing cohesion and the Soviet Union was no longer guiding all other Communist countries. Communism ceased to be a closed camp. The power of China, the Sino-Soviet dispute, and the rebellions in East Germany, Poland, Hungary, and Czechoslovakia had much to do with the decline of Soviet supremacy. Communist countries began to follow their own "road to socialism" — meaning that they were interpreting Marxism in the light of their national history, the type of civilization they had, and the stage of their industrial development.

In the 1970s, on lines similar to those taken earlier by the Yugoslav party, a number of major Western European Communist parties have been adopting a liberal and independent approach to politics known as Eurocommunism. These parties are abandoning two fundamental Marxist notions: proletarian internationalism and the need for a dictatorship of the proletariat. They proclaim their belief in the democratic road to communism — that is, to rule only when, and only for as long as, they recieve the support of the majority in free elections. They also profess a commitment to civil liberties and promise that there shall be no violation of human rights in the name socialism. While they are in power, complete freedom of expression for all currents of scientific, philosophical, cultural, and artistic expression will be preserved. The Eurocommunists argue that their road will lead to a higher form of socialism and the "active participation of everyone". They are demanding from the Soviet Union reciprocal respect for different roads to communism and are seeking merely an identity of views among all Communist parties on the basis of fraternal friendship in the struggle for social change of a "progressive nature".*

Notwithstanding changed circumstances, there is an enduring confrontation with the rest of the world. In 1968 Soviet leader Leonid Brezhnev laid down what became known as the Brezhnev Doctrine. He proclaimed that the Soviet Union was entitled to intervene militarily (as it did in Hungary and Czechoslovakia) in any Communist country in which there was a threat of the restoration of capitalism. Moreover, while carefully avoiding the risk of war, the Soviet Union is seeking to encroach the non-Communist world. In 1976, referring to the official quest of a détente — that is, a lessening of tensions — with the United States and other Western countries, Brezhnev declared that détente was not an end in itself but a means of achieving the Soviet Union's strategic objectives. Détente merely meant that disputes and conflicts between countries would not be settled by the use or threat of arms. It did not "in the slightest abolish, and cannot abolish or alter, the laws of the class struggle". Brezhnev also stated that the Soviet Union had the right to support "the struggle of other peoples for freedom and progress". It would seem that a

---

* In the Western countries, doubts are expressed about the sincerity of the Eurocommunists. It is widely felt that once they enter government — by playing on the pacifist, neutralist, and nationalist emotions — they will destroy the existing political, military, and economic co-operation of the Western world. In the Soviet Union, on the other hand, the view may well be held that eventually the Eurocommunists will have to resort to violence to counter the violence of the reactionaries and establish the dictatorship of the proletariat. Once that crucial stage is reached, they will have to accept a truly revolutionary character.

system of government that has to justify its policies theoretically in Marxist-Leninist terms cannot abstain from giving — under the banner of socialism or anti-imperialism — moral, political and material support to local wars of "national liberation" or any other revolutionary upheavals in other countries.

The Soviet Union perseveres with a duality of foreign policy objectives. Ever since 1917 it has pursued two contradictory aims: on the one hand it has attempted to safeguard its national interests by establishing peaceful relations with non-Communist countries, and on the other hand it has tried to promote revolution in these countries. At any given time, one or the other of these goals predominate, but at no stage has one of them been completely dormant. The Soviet Union is caught in a position between a militant ideology and a practical reality.

Marxism in China

From the fifth century until modern times, China was technically the most advanced country in the world. At one stage she ruled over the largest empire the world has ever known. But the scholarly bureaucrats who ran China's affairs in accordance with the Confucian philosophy did not emulate the Industrial Revolution that was sweeping Western Europe during the eighteenth and nineteenth centuries. They regarded tranquillity and order, not struggle and change, as the primary goals of society. Because they chose to ignore the military and political realities emerging around them, and left the control of China's armed power in the hands of feudal militarists who protected their personal interests rather than the interests of the country, China was weak and everybody's prey. Beginning with the Opium War of 1838-40, China was subjugated by, singly and collectively, European, American, and Japanese military strength. As time passed, it became increasingly evident that — if China were not to sink into utter dependence and helplessness — fundamental changes would have to take place.

In 1911 an essentailly bourgeois democratic revolution

overthrew the old regime. But no significant national capitalist class could come into being, because the Western countries wanted China to remain a market for their goods. The import duties China was allowed to levy by unequal treaties were too low to enable an agrarian economy to establish an industrial base. In an industrially backward country it is hard for an industry to survive its initial difficulties if on the home market it is exposed to practically free competition from long-established foreign firms.

During the First World War the political and economic stranglehold was relaxed, and China, being promised that the treaties imposed on her would be revised, entered the war. Because these promises were not honoured at the Peace Conference of Versailles — and this decision was meekly accepted by the Chinese delegation — there were massive student demonstrations on 4 May 1919, followed by marches and strikes in about two hundred cities and towns. Those who took part were not only students and workers but also teachers, professors, shopkeepers, and merchants. For the first time in the history of modern China, progressive elements had succeeded in inspiring and organizing a mass movement. The centre of this ferment, known as the May Fourth Movement, was the Peking National University.

A young teacher called Mao Tse-tung* was employed as a librarian's assistant at the Peking University. He was an avid reader of Western books on philosophy, history, politics and economics and participated in the discussions of the "Marxist study group" at the university. In 1921 he was one of the twelve young men who founded the Chinese Communist Party. All had participated in the May Fourth Movement and had been influenced by it. Probably they knew only little about Marx's doctrine, because at the time hardly any Marxist literature had been translated into Chinese, but they turned to Marxism when the Russian revolution seemed to point the

---

* China decided to use, as from 1 January 1979, its own phonetic alphabet to standardize the romanization of Chinese names of persons and places. In the index the reader can find in brackets after the entry the new spelling of the Chinese names that appear in this book.

way to a possible solution of China's weaknesses and insta-
bility caused by the combination of feudalism, bureaucracy,
and imperialist capitalism.

In 1922, under pressure from the Third International, the
Communists began to co-operate with the "bourgeois
nationalist" government to bring to a head the "national revolution" that would lead to the unity of China and her independence. This was seen as being a part in the world-wide
revolution destined to destroy imperialism and bring about the
overthrow of capitalism in Europe and elsewhere. By 1925, the
party had grown in membership from a few dozen in 1921 to
tens of thousands, and, feeling stronger, the Communists
began to speak more openly about their aims. These were to
participate in the national-revolutionary government and to
use its state and military apparatuses as instruments of achieving hegemony. To put it more bluntly, they were to enter the
government in order to take it over — and not to play a
secondary role as was favoured at the time by Moscow.

Since most of the officers in the army came from landlord
and well-to-do families, a strong right-wing opposition to the
Communists developed. In 1927 the government decided to
move before the Communists became too strong. In April,
during the so-called white terror, four-fifths of the party's
membership were massacred in Shanghai. This ended all collaboration between the government and the Communists, and
the Central Committee of the Communist Party sent Mao to
Hunan, where the peasants showed signs of awakening to political activity. By adapting the slogans of the day to appeal to
the peasant mentality, Mao managed to organize a worker-
peasant army and, between July and September, led them in
the Autumn Harvest Uprising. It ended in defeat and sparked
off another massacre of the Communists.

With a few hundred survivors, Mao fled to the mountains
of south-west Kiangsi. Here they were joined by other fugi-
tives and united with two bandit chiefs who were already
established in this remote region.* This brought his forces up

* During the whole of the civil war, Mao was ready to accept the support of
bandits and other outcasts. This was not only because he needed more men

to sixteen hundred men, who were called the Red Army. By 1929, similar red bases were established in half a dozen places across China. The Red Army consisted of well-disciplined bands that conducted guerilla warfare. In order to ensure themselves of the support of the peasantry — and in sharp contrast to the predatory armies of the warlords and the government — they neither plundered nor commandeered food without payment. Mao knew that the sympathy of the peasant masses was indispensable to the success of his guerilla activities and, indeed, to the eventual victory of the Communist revolution.

At first, within the areas under their control, the Communists confiscated the whole of the land and then divided it up among the peasants. This policy met with strong opposition from the peasants. The peasants in general were deeply attached to their little plots and hostile to its confiscation even in those cases where the land allocated to them in exchange was larger and more fertile. In 1929 this policy was changed: only the estates of the landlords were confiscated. Land reform became a political as much as an economic measure. The landlord class was declared to be the principal enemy of the revolution and had to be eliminated. The confiscation of their property not only destroyed the economic basis for their existence as a class but also involved the peasant masses in a "class struggle" against their former exploiters. It was a process of revolutionary education: the peasantry was being awakened "to a consciousness of their true interests". As the better-off peasants were left alone, the new policy also had the advantage of antagonizing only a small percentage of the total rural population.

Until 1931, Mao could act more or less according to his understanding of what must be done. The written instructions he received from the Central Committee — which operated clandestinely in Shanghai — could be circumvented by delaying tactics. The situation changed when the Central Committee decided to exchange its hunted existence in Shanghai

but also because he had some sympathy with these old-fashioned rebels and thought it possible that, through "intensive education", they could be transformed into true revolutionaries.

for the relative security of the base area in Kiangsi. In November 1931 it proclaimed a Chinese Soviet Republic in the areas the Communists controlled — with Kiangsi as the central soviet area.

Mao's authority was gradually reduced, and by 1933 he had even lost control over his armies. Two outside events had a bearing on this. One was the onset of the Sino-Japanese conflict; the other was the economic depression in the Western countries, which encouraged the belief that a "revolutionary upsurge" was growing out of the "sharpening of the general crisis of capitalism". Both events were seen as signs that the time had come for the Communists to act more positively. And there was another factor: the Red Army had grown in strength. It had close to three hundred thousand men, of whom about eighty thousand were in the central area in Kiangsi. Mao's "guerillaism" — that is, the tactic of luring the enemy forces deep into soviet territory and attacking them piecemeal by surprise with a larger force — was denounced as inadequate. Instead the Central Committee decided upon what it called a "forward and offensive line" — meaning that it would take the fight outside the soviet areas and conduct warfare on the basis of equality. This strategy was to have the added advantage of putting an end to the situation in which the population of the soviet areas were the constant victims of the civil war.

But the government forces had also changed their tactics. Instead of conducting campaigns against the soviet areas, they built a chain of blockhouses linked by barbed wire around the soviet area in Kiangsi. This not only made it more difficult for the Red Army to move out of its area to attack the enemy but also made it possible for the government to enforce a strict economic blockade. The latter had a devastating effect. Food prices began to rise at a very fast rate, and an acute shortage of salt for the population developed. As the situation deteriorated, the Communists decided to give up their base in Kiangsi. This move was justified with the explanation that the Red Army was transferring north to fight the Japanese.

Thus in 1934 started the legendary heroic Long March of about ten thousand kilometres over mountainous terrain and treacherous swamplands. As it also involved fighting off the enemy along the route, the Long March is one of the great feats in military history. Of the estimated hundred thousand men, women, and children who left Kiangsi, only about eight thousand survived the ordeal and arrived, one year later, in North Shensi.

During the Long March, Mao Tse-tung was elected to the newly created post of chairman of the Chinese Communist Party. This made him the unchallengeable leader and the symbol of the movement itself. With the thirty thousand men under his control (others had joined them since they left Kiangsi), he began to establish new bases both to continue the civil war and to fight the Japanese. In 1937 Yenan, a small provincial town, became his headquarters; the next ten years or so are known as the Yenan Period.

The Communists obtained the goodwill of the peasants in their area by restricting rent payments to no more than one-third of their crop, setting up mutual-aid teams, and getting them politically involved by holding village elections. They had no difficulty in finding new recruits from among the very poor peasantry of northern China.

At Yenan, Mao was at last able to assimilate more fully the basic principles of Marxism-Leninism. As the Third International ceased to hold congresses after 1935, he was no longer "meddled with" in policy formulation. This made it easier for him to choose from the Marxist-Leninist philosophy what he regarded as useful to an ideology adapted to the Chinese conditions and to discard the rest. While he accepted Marxism-Leninism as a universal and immutable "fundamental theory", at the same time he saw his revolution as a logical successor of the peasant upheavals that had shaken China through two thousand years. He argued that a revolutionary leader must be flexible and capable of learning lessons from the historical development of his society. Mao seemed particularly worried about dogmatism and the grip Marxist fundamentalists might gain on the revolution. In 1938 he laid down that a Communist was a Marxist internationalist, but Marxism had to take on a national form before it could be applied. "There is no such thing as abstract Marxism," he said, "but only concrete Marxism that has taken on a national form. . . We must discard our dogmatism and replace it by a new and vital Chinese style and manner, pleasing to the eye and to the ear of the Chinese common people."

In other words, theory had to be "correctly" integrated with the concrete situation in China at the time. Because theory and practice had to be co-ordinated to meet the needs of the situation as they presented themselves, one had always to test theory against objective reality. This line of reasoning enabled Mao to declare that in the Communist revolution the peasants were not auxiliaries and could be even more "uncompromisingly revolutionary" than the urban workers. As long as the Communists were leading the peasant rebellion, the Marxist-Leninist principles were being maintained. Thus, as in Russia, the Marxist theory was made to conform to the facts of the situation.

In 1937 the civil war was suspended in order to unify the struggle against the Japanese. In northern and eastern China the Communists, although under the nominal control of the government, fought an independent war. They resorted to their customary guerilla tactics of "avoiding strength and striking at weaknesses". They not only concentrated their own forces to destroy small enemy units but regarded the killing of enemy soldiers as more important than the conquest of territory or strong points. Because the Japanese army recognized the danger of being overextended and held on to only the larger cities and the railways that connected them, the Red Army dominated the countryside.

The success of the guerilla warfare and their honest administration and moderate economic policies earned the Communists the respect of a large segment of the Chinese population. This enabled them to mobilize, for their purposes, the patriotic sentiments released by the continuing Japanese aggression. They appealed to all classes, in the name of unity against the invaders, and drew a large number of new recruits — including students and intellectuals — from the coastal cities. When the Japanese surrendered in 1945, the Communists not only completely occupied their areas — bringing more than a quarter of the Chinese people under their immediate political control — but also enjoyed widespread support in the rest of China. The national government, which had to rely on warlords, landlords, and the small manufacturing class to fight both the Communists and the Japanese invaders, had degenerated into ruling in these people's interests. High rents, black marketeering, corruption, and a rampant inflation had helped to fill their pockets while millions of peasants starved. As a result, when the civil war was resumed, the Communists were able to win it by 1949.

During the years of struggle, thousands of landlords had been killed by the peasants. This helped to clear the way for the new society: the People's Republic of China, with Mao Tse-tung at its head. The war-weary Chinese people, enthusiastically or tacitly, welcomed their new rulers. And, as the people had a deep longing for stable and efficient government, the country settled down.

In his celebrated essay *On the People's Democratic Dictatorship*, published in June 1949, Mao set down his long-range objectives: China was "to advance steadily, under the leadership of the working class and the Communist Party, from an agricultural to an industrial country, from a new democracy to a socialist and eventually communist society, to abolish classes and to establish world communism". Mao used the term *new democracy* to distinguish this stage from the "old" bourgeois-democratic revolution. The difference between the two was that it would be led not by the bourgeoisie alone but by the "joint revolutionary-democratic dictatorship of several revolutionary classes" — hence "people's democratic dictatorship". This fitted in with the Marxist-Leninist principle that a pre-capitalist society, such as China, must pass through a "bourgeois-democratic" revolution before it could have a socialist one.

According to Mao, the "people" — defined as an alliance between the workers, the peasants, and the "national bourgeoisie" who enjoyed democratic rights — were to impose their dictatorship over the "reactionaries". The latter comprised the landlord class and the "bureaucratic bourgeoisie" — meaning that segment of the population that was linked to the previous regime. During the people's democratic dictatorship, the reactionary classes were to be eliminated; a number of their members were to be put to death while the rest were to be reduced to the status of manual labourers. The "people's state apparatuses" would be strengthened in order to serve more efficiently as the instrument for the transformation and elimination of the "antagonistic classes".

One of the first major internal measures taken by the new rulers was to replace misrule and corruption with Communist discipline and organization. Street committees were set up — that is, people were made responsible for policing their own streets. Another measure taken was to promulgate a new law of marriage. It abolished the practice of parents arranging the marriage of their children and gave them the right to choose their own partners. The law also gave equal rights in the home to both partners. Women were liberated from their former rulers: their fathers, husbands, and mothers-in-law. This brought to an end the system of extended family that had existed for thousands of years and weakened the hold the family had over the individual. And women, being made equal to men in every respect, were placed in a position in which they could serve the new order on an equal footing.

The education system and the media, as well as the police and the judiciary, were placed under the control of the Communist Party. All large businesses were nationalized, while the smaller businesses came under "state-private" management — meaning that they were owned by the state but the former owners continued in the capacity of salaried managers and were also entitled to a 5 per cent return on their investment. In line with the Agrarian Reform Act of 1950, the lands of the landlords not yet confiscated — because they were not in the areas "liberated" by the Red Army during the civil war — were divided into small plots and distributed among the tenants, poor peasants, and farm labourers. These reforms were carried out with haste, and often with revolutionary terror, by the peasant cadres that won the civil war. Former landlords were accused and their "crimes" exposed in people's tribunals manned by peasants. Those found to have committed crimes, other than the usual exploitation, were executed or sentenced to an indefinite period of detention

during which their thinking would be reformed; the others were put on probation "under the supervision of the masses" and received their share of land to work.

But the land reforms carried out in the years 1950 to 1952 were merely meant to complete the "class struggle" designed to eliminate feudal landlordism initiated in 1929. They were followed by the collectivization of agriculture. While industry was said to be the leading factor in the socialist economy, agriculture was described as its base. No industry can develop without a reliable source of food and raw materials. It followed that China could break out of its backwardness only through the transformation of the countryside; and only under collectivization could the feudal peasant become literate and able to understand scientific methods. Moreover, collectivization would "minimize or abolish the difference between country and city, between rural and factory work, between manual and mental labour". From 1952 onwards, through mutual-aid teams, lower co-operatives (in which deeds were held privately), then higher co-operatives (in which deeds were burned and villagers pooled their land and tools), collectivization proceeded step by step. Collectivization not only allowed for more rational farming on a large scale but also prevented the peasantry from growing into a new landlord class.

At first, collectivization led to a deterioration in agriculture. Slaughter of farm animals and the destruction of trees and crops were widespread. In 1955 acute food shortages were reported. However, as the Chinese peasants had held the land for only a few years, their reaction to collectivization was not as desperate as it had been in Russia, where the peasants' ties to their land were more traditional.

By 1956, 95 per cent of the peasant population was already in collectives. Each collective was an integrated socioeconomic unit, villagers holding the land in collective ownership and working it as a unit. And each collective was operating within the framework of the planned national economy.

Soon after the Communists had assumed power, they had inaugurated a nationwide socialist education programme. At first it affected chiefly the intellectuals — that is, the professional class, the civil service, and a small segment of the urban grating the universal truth of Marxism-Leninism not only with the concrete situation in China but also with the concrete situation of an era in which imperialism was heading towards total collapse and socialism was advancing to world-wide victory. The teachings of Chairman Mao were described as the summit of Marxism-Leninism in our time. By bringing Marxism-Leninism to a higher and completely new stage, they were the best and most efficient guide on how to think correctly. The intensive study of Mao Tse-tung Thought was said to raise dedication and determination. Apart from exhorting people to struggle relentlessly against imperialism and revisionism, it affirmed the power of the human will and demonstrated that the difficulties encountered in the path of economic development could be solved by examining mistakes and drawing lessons from them, and by meeting failure with new determination.

The Constitution of the Chinese People's Republic, adopted in 1954, announced in its preamble that the necessary conditions had been created for "planned economic construction and gradual transition to socialism". By this time the first five-year plan had started, and practically every aspect of Chinese life had come to be organized and supervised by the Chinese Communist Party. The "new democracy" stage being over and China having officially entered the "socialist" stage, party members — numbering about ten million in 1956, eighteen million in 1965, and thirty-five million in 1977 — became the "vanguards of the dictatorship of the proletariat". In theory, the leading body of the Party is the National Party Congress, which is meant to be convened at least once every five years. It elects the Central Committee, composed of about two hundred members, from which the twenty-three members of the Political Bureau are chosen. In practice, the Central Committee follows the lind laid down by the Political Bureau, and party congresses are convened irregularly to approve new policies decided at the top. These policies are carried out through a network of regional, provisional, and municipal organizations and committees of peasants, workers, youths, women, and others. Party members take command of these committees and direct them both in their work and in their struggle against the "enemies of the proletariat and the people".

It is argued that as China is still passing through the Socialist stage of development, the party must persevere with the dictatorship of the proletariat. And not only because there are still reactionary elements within society — clinging to old ideas, customs, and values — who must be remoulded into new men, but also because there are still different types of relations to the means of production. First, there is "socialist" ownership — that is, ownership by the whole of the people — of the manufacturing industry; second, there is "semi-socialist" collective ownership in the agricultural and handcraft co-operatives; and third, there is some private ownership in small-scale modes of production. Because not all the means of production are as yet owned by the whole of the people, there are still class differences between the workers and the peasants and between them and the national bourgeoisie. And, where there are class differences, a class struggle exists. As the class struggle in China will not disappear for a long time, there can be no transition to the higher stage of communism.

A member of the Chinese Communist Party is expected to subordinate his personal interests and private life to the party. By preference he is recruited from among the literate young workers and peasants. The policy is to keep the membership of the party young because, in middle age, people tend more towards routine than progress. A party member must be "boundlessly loyal" to the people and serve them wholeheartedly without calculation of gain or loss. The slogan is: "Forget yourself; serve the people" — by continuously remoulding them and consolidating the proletarian ranks, and thus build up socialism and effect the transition to communism. At the same time, a party member is asked to integrate Marxism-Leninism with the concrete facts he encounters — that is, temper ideological convictions if the situation facing him demands it. He should be attuned to the public's needs and not move too far ahead of them. He should never become complacent or arrogant in power, and he should always practise what he teaches.

Marx's historical evolutionary theory fell on fertile ground in China. Dialectic thinking — that is, the concept of the centrality of contradictions in the evolution of nature and society — is rooted in traditional Chinese philosophy. Contradictions are seen as the fuel that keeps everything in motion: the resolution of a contradiction brings progress — and new opposition. As contradictions are everywhere, one must constantly take sides. But the traditional Chinese understanding of the dialectic pattern is essentially different from that of Hegel and Marx. Contradictions are not seen as a source of forward movement propelling humanity towards a state of permanent Utopia. Except time and space, nothing is infinite. All things have a beginning and an end. There is a perpetual decline and renewal; a flux between haste and deliberation, toil and rest, reality and dream, and so on. Contradictions constitute a unity of opposites, as in birth and death. Grain is born once a year and dies once a year, and the more that dies the more is born. Because contradictions are the life-blood of reality, there is a continuous state of change that cannot come to a stop.

In his philosophical essay entitled *On Contradictions*, written in 1937, Mao stressed the universality of contradictions and analysed them on three levels. The first is within the individual where there is a contradiction between the old and the new; the second is within society between the rich and the poor and between the city and the country; and the third is the global contradiction between socialism and capitalism. But, in line with traditional Chinese thinking, Mao did not believe that the reconciliation of these contradictions would lead to a complete and final harmony once communism was established throughout the world. He accepted the notion of a "permanent revolution" — though based on a different set of assumptions from that propagated by Trotsky. As he was to explain in 1958: "Capitalism leads to socialism, socialism leads to communism, and Communist society must still be re-formed. It will have a beginning and an end. It will certainly be divided into stages, or they will give it a different name. It cannot remain constant." This is because if "there were no contradictions and no struggle, there would be no world, no progress, no life; there would be nothing at all."

In 1957, in his speech "On the Correct Handling of Contradictions among the People", Mao developed the idea of two types of contradictions: antagonistic and non-antagonistic.

Antagonistic contradictions are those between Socialist and capitalist societies and, within Socialist countries, between the revolutionaries and the counter-revolutionaries. Antagonistic contradictions cannot be resolved peacefully; moral coercion and sometimes force are required. Non-antagonistic contradictions occur among those who disagree with the methods but not the aims of socialism. These are contradictions "among the people". Because "socialist society grows more united through the ceaseless process of carefully dealing and resolving contradictions", it is the task of the leadership to resolve these ever-present non-antagonistic contradictions among the people.

The correct way of dealing with contradictions, so as to achieve ideological consolidation and Socialist progress, is by "discussion and criticism or persuasion and education". A continuous "thought struggle" must be waged to eradicate all the vestiges of feudal and capitalist thinking. This leads to an awareness within the framework of the guiding principles of Marxism-Leninism.

In line with Mao Tse-tung's thinking, within the party, the bureaucracy, and the army there was in existence a continuous and painstaking process of ideological remoulding. From time to time there were intensive shake-ups known as "rectification" campaigns. The most important was the Great Rectification of 1942-44 at Yenan. At this stage — because unity and discipline had to be strengthened in very difficult circumstances — there was some physical liquidation, but after that, re-education and labour under supervision were the primary tools of persuasion. Mao had come to believe that only the force of ideas, and not crude and coercive methods, would bring about a change "within the soul of man" and the ideological unity of the people.

In 1956 Mao stated that it could not be said that all their intellectuals had yet "achieved remoulding. Only about 40 per cent could be called progressive." Because Socialist construction could not proceed without the intellectuals, in 1957 a "non-antagonistic struggle" was initiated. It was called Blooming and Contending — a name derived from a classical call for philosophical debate, "Let a hundred flowers bloom and a hundred schools of thought contend". The intellectuals were invited to criticize the party and the government in order to assess the tendencies among them, expose legitimate grievances, and — by correcting "incorrect thought" — guide them towards socialism. This rectification process was expected to induce them to contribute more of their scientific, technical, and creative skills to the nation and also to establish a greater unity between them and the masses.

At first the movement drew only slow response. However, upon repeated urgings, intellectuals, lecturers, teachers, and students began voicing opinions. But instead of raising only minor matters such as abuse of power, incompetence, corruption, and so on, they questioned fundamental issues. For instance, they wanted to know why there was so little freedom in choosing candidates for various offices, whether the dictatorship of the proletariat was really justified once the exploiting classes had been abolished, and how was it possible for Stalin to commit so many atrocities in a socialist country. This type of questioning, without actually attacking communism as an ideology, grew into a display of dissatisfaction.

When it seemed to the leadership that matters threatened to get out of hand, an Anti-Rightist Movement was initiated. In endless nerve-racking meetings, and in article after afticle, critics were denounced as "rightists" and accused of wanting to overthrow the party and the dictatorship of the proletariat in order to seize power for themselves instead of assisting unification. The gap between the intellectuals and the people had grown too wide. The intellectuals had to be "struggled against": criticized and thrown together with the masses. Many were removed from positions of responsibility, and the younger and less well-known rightists were sent to villages and into factories to reform themselves through physical labour. Mao became suspicious of all those who had a bourgeois background. He had concluded that, despite persistent remoulding attempts, many of them were not only unreformed but also unrepentent reactionaries. Because they could not be trusted, they had to be watched continuously and, if necessary, replaced — preferably by people who had their roots among the masses.

The lessons learned by the Chinese leadership from the experiences of the rectification campaign appear to have been that it could afford neither liberalization at home nor a relaxation of the struggle abroad. It imposed a stricter control over the Chinese people; all interplay of ideas that did not serve the revolution was suppressed. While discussion and criticism were allowed, they had to be conducted along the Mao-inspired "general line" of constructing socialism. Only flowers of the right red hue were permitted to bloom. And, if at home many of the bourgeois did not change, how could one expect a conversion in non-Communist countries? The reactionaries would relinquish their powers only after protracted struggle, and China must prepare for it.

In 1958 the Chinese leadership embarked upon a policy of mobilizing the masses for what was to be the Great Leap Forward. Its stated aim was to "catch up with England in fifteen years" — meaning to produce 40 million tons of steel annually instead of merely just over 5 million tons. In other words, it was decided to speed up the pace of economic progress to catch up with the industrially advanced countries in a relatively short time.

To meet the challenge, collectives were amalgamated into "people's communes". About twenty-four thousand such communes were established, each composed of about five thousand households representing on the average twenty-five thousand people. The communes were made responsible for production, education, health, and social services, and all construction work within the area. Under the new system, peasants could be directed to work outside their villages and to be involved in small-scale manufacture and handicrafts. Once the harvest was in, they were asked to produce pig-iron and steel in small backyard furnaces. In this way the peasants, instead of working only 120 to 150 days a year, could be employed in productive work for most of the year.

Durig the period of the Great Leap Forward, millions of city people were dispatched to the country. They were employed in road building, in the construction of irrigation channels and dams, in terracing farmlands in mountainous regions, in increasing fertilizer resources, and in small farm-servicing industries. People were driven by party members to labour long hours with only two days rest a month. Often husband and wife worked in different places and had to eat in common mess halls while their children were placed in nurseries. Revolutionary enthusiam and ideological purity, and not technical expertise and the resources available, determined what had to be done. Planning was pushed aside; it was argued that too many plans and blueprints lead only to bureaucratization and the retardation of progress. Because party members overreached themselves in enthusiasm and drive, while lacking experience, too much was attempted in a random way. Excessively deep ploughing and close planting were introduced. Many factories were built for which there was no machinery. Roads were constructed by labour recruited from villages while the harvest went rotting on the ground. In an effort to show results, quality was sacrificed to quantity. Bottlenecks developed everywhere. The situation was aggravated by the shortage of transportation available in China. Food and other supplies could not be taken from areas with a surplus to those with a deficiency.

The great waste of resources demoralized workers, technicians, and managers alike. Discontent was rife. Apart from widespread resistance and sabotage, the country had to endure droughts, floods, and associated plant diseases. By 1959 there was a serious shortage of food in many parts of China. Only an extremely efficient rationing system prevented famines and mass starvation, but not widespread malnutrition. In 1960, especially after the Russian experts were recalled and the Soviet Union repudiated all contracts and stopped supplying spare parts and equipment, factory after factory had to close down and projects under construction had to be abandoned. After another disastrous harvest, whole areas degenerated into lawlessness and had to be controlled by the military. China faced a crisis that reached its peak during the 1961/62 winter.

The Great Leap Forward — an experiment unparalleled in modern history — was wound up. It had turned the country upside down, but it was not just a waste. It is reported that, in 1958, 150,000 kilometres of new roads and 30,000 kilometres of new railways were built, five rivers were linked by canals, eighty thousand small mines developed, and a number of major projects — such as irrigation schemes and dams to control floods — were completed. It also laid the foundation for the creation of a steel industry in every commune throughout China. But its greatest benefit is believed to be that it made the peasants more aware of technology.

Mao Tse-tung, who appeared chastened by what happened, chose to withdraw temporarily from public view. He resigned from the position of president of the republic (the government branch of rule) but remained the chairman of the Chinese Communist Party — the most powerful position in China. The party elected its vice-chairman, Liu Shao-chi — who was the designated successor to Mao — as the new president of the republic. He adopted a more pragmatic approach towards both economic policy and propaganda. During the period that followed the "three bad years", policy was "to keep one eye shut and one eye open". This allowed administrative power to be divided once again into "experts" and "reds".

In the rural areas the ownership of most of the means of production reverted from the communes to the collectives. The collectives were reduced to a more manageable size of about a hundred households, with the result that, instead of each village forming one collective, large villages comprised two or more collectives. The communes were also reduced in size.* Taxes on peasants were eased, and more consumer

---

* At the time of writing there were about fifty thousand communes in China, with about thirteen thousand people in each. They form a regional administrative network, responsible for the general welfare of their members. They run lower-grade and even some middle-grade schools, libraries, hospitals, clinics, veterinary stations, and agricultural research stations. They are in charge of planning within their area, organize relief when harvests fail, and call upon people to labour outside their villages in the case of an emergency such as flood control. While the collectives are the unit for the common ownership of the means of production, the basic accounting unit in rural China is the production team. There are some five million production teams — the typical production team consists of about thirty households or 150 people, which is the average size of a small village. As the members share in the income of their team, there is collective interest in the harvest; and there are highly disparate incomes between the members of one team and those of another.

goods of the type normally purchased by villagers were produced. Backyard furnaces, because of the very poor quality on their output, were abandoned except in those places where this kind of activity had good prospects. Family ownership of farmhouses came to be guaranteed in the sense that families, while they owned their houses and paid no rent, could not sell or rent them to others. Individual households were also given small garden plots for private cultivation and encouraged to raise goats, chickens, sheep, and pigs. Peasants were also asked to produce such goods as sweaters and baskets at home. Urban free markets and rural fairs were opened under official supervision; there people could sell their surplus output outside the marketing co-operatives and other regular state channels of trade. Small-scale non-agricultural private enterprises — doctors, barbers, shoe-repairers, curio dealers, and the like — were also more openly tolerated so long as they occasioned "no exploitation of others". In industry, bonus systems and other material incentives were introduced.

By 1963 China had recovered from what some had described as her "magnificent madness". The harvest was good and the production level had again reached what it was before the Great Leap Forward. In 1964 there was a small surplus in meat, eggs, and vegetables. When the economic equilibrium was restored, the people's confidence in the leadership and the party returned.

But Liu Shao-chi was taking the country further and further away from the path of "democratic centralism". This idea of democratic centralism formed part of Marx's vision of the future society. As noted earlier, a kind of democratic centralism was applied by Lenin within the Russian party. It meant, very broadly, that there were to be "democratic" consultations with the rank and file of the party but absolute submission once a decision was reached at the centre. Mao Tsetung took the view that, in order to achieve a lasting radical transformation of society, democratic centralism should not be limited to the cadres but should be extended to the whole of the people. The masses should be consulted. People should be encouraged to speak out on all important matters, and different opinions, should be listened to seriously and analysed.

Those who had incorrect thoughts should be taught and transformed in order to enable them to follow the general line. Only when people felt that they were actively involved in shaping their fate would they be subsequently in the right frame of mind to accept willingly and wholeheartedly the decisions of the leadership. And only by mobilizing the revolutionary enthusiasm of the masses would the country be in a position to overcome the many difficulties encountered in the path of socialist construction. It would release not only the energy of the whole population but also the talent and initiative of each individual. While Mao believed in this mass-line method, Liu was leaning strongly towards hierarchical control directed from the centre. He saw democracy and centralism as contradictory concepts too difficult to reconcile.

This caused Mao to become apprehensive that the momentum of his revolution aimed at establishing a truly Communist society was slowing to a standstill and that China might be taking the road back to capitalism. He knew, as Marx had stressed, that it was not enough to abolish private property to establish communism — the entire bourgeois cultural superstructure had to be replaced as well. Many times in history successful revolutions had been followed by the restoration of the old order. Moreover, the "revisionist road" taken by the Soviet Union and other socialist countries, and the inroads of revisionism into every Communist party in the world, were horrid examples of what Mao feared might happen in China.

Men in their forties and fifties, who were recruited as young people after the Communists came to power, had assumed entrenched positions within the immense bureaucratic structure. Mao's contempt for and distrust of bureaucracy are well known. He regarded bureaucrats, and more specifically middle-aged bureaucrats, as people who had a vested interest in the *status quo* and who ignored the long-term ideological implications of their decisions and actions. They tended to look at their functions from a purely administrative, professional, or technical point of view and were insensitive to the general needs of society. They were more interested in things than they were in people. By having lost their revolutionary zeal, they were diverting the nation from building a new China.

Apart from being concerned about the danger of bureaucratic calcification, Mao was also worried about who were going to be the successors of the existing leadership and about the trend towards "élitism". The failure of the Great Leap Forward (by this time entirely blamed on the droughts and the Russian withdrawal of technical assistance) had enabled revisionists and other "representatives of the old and new bourgoisie", and the "loiterers at the cross-roads", to attain high places in the party and government. In short, once the ageing revolutionary leadership passed away, the wrong people might seize power.

The question therefore was how to rekindle the revolutionary fires, how to bring the spirit of the revolution to the new generation in whose hands the future lay, and how to teach them to consolidate the dictatorship of the proletariat and to put such pressures on those in authority that they would never dare to deviate from the road that would carry the revolution to its destination.

In 1963, in order to put China back on his socialist road and to "train and bring up millions of successors who will carry on the cause of the proletarian revolution", Mao instigated the Socialist Education Movement. It was first implemented in the army under the direction of Lin Piao — the minister of defence. To unify ideological training, Lin Piao compiled the famous "little red book" — a distilled version of Mao Tse-tung Thought — which was distributed to all army personnel for intense study. Moreover, to enforce more fully Mao's egalitarian ideas, all rank insignia and all differences in uniforms between officers and soldiers were abolished. In 1965, when the Movement was taken into the rural areas and from there into the cities, army cadres assisted in the spreading of the "great school of Mao Tse-tung Thought". This revived the army's revolutionary tradition of close involvement in civil affairs and political struggles.

In the beginning, the Socialist Education Movement was a relatively tame affair. To bring home to the young generation — who had grown up since 1949 — the lessons of past hardships and struggles, statues of clay and lifelike representations of heart-breaking scenes of the past were exhibited. Plays, dramas, and stories concentrated on the themes "Do not forget the bad old days" and "Never forget the class struggle". But as time passed, the movement was radicalized. Attacks on "right-leaning elements" grew in intensity. The rightists were accused of putting personal interests ahead of the collective interest and thus undermining the co-operative spirit of the proletarian revolution. By having given private plots of land and outlets where individual households could sell their surplus products in conditions of a free market, and by encouraging other capitalist practices such as bonuses and piecework, they were sowing counter-revolutionary seeds. Material reward, instead of social effort, was becoming the criterion of success. Moreover, by insisting upon the need for organization and authority, the rightists had developed superior attitudes towards the people and carried out their work in an undemocratic manner. They relied on experts and subordinated the workers to the technicians. They showed love for rank, status, and power and took advantage of their position to gain privileges and amenities for themselves. In short, a "new class" was being created — an élite of power wielders, divorced from labour and the people, who followed a revisionist road to capitalism.

But, particularly in the cities, the Movement was either blocked or ignored with the tacit consent of many of those in authority. Mao realized that, despite the widespread personality cult he was subject to at the time, he was losing control over much of the party and propaganda machinery. In order to recover full authority, he decided to purge those "in authority who were taking the capitalist road" and all their accomplices in the lower ranks. Because these people were too well entrenched, and opposition proved more widely spread and powerful than he had imagined, it became necessary that he should involve the masses. As he had the full support of the army, Mao knew that there would be no danger of a coup against his leadership.

On 16 May 1966, the Central Commitee of the Chinese Communist Party formally launched the Great Proletarian Cultural Revolution. The committee issued a circular informing the people that the views and policies of Chairman Mao were being flouted by individuals in positions of high authority. In the circular, the Central Committee called upon the Cultural Revolution to pound at "the decadent ideological and cultural position still held by the bourgeoisie and the remnants of feudalism" and to weed out "those representatives of the bourgeoisie who had sneaked into the Communist Party". It pointed out: "Although the bourgeoisie has been overthrown, it is still trying to use the old ideas, culture, customs, and habits of the exploiting classes to corrupt the masses, capture their minds, and endeavour to stage a comeback. The proletariat must do the exact opposite: it must meet head-on every challenge of the bourgeoisie in the ideological field and use the new ideas, culture, customs, and habits of the proletariat to change the mental outlook of the whole society."

The most dangerous "black line" (meaning revisionist, in contrast to the correct "red line") of development was in the fields of art, culture, and education. Consequently, the first and one of the most important tasks of the Cultural Revolution was to "reform the old system of education, as well as the principles and methods of teaching". "Academic power cliques" within educational institutions were described as bourgeois strongholds whose influence had to be broken. It was stressed that it was "through schools that the proletariat trains and cultivates its successors and through schools, too, that the bourgeoisie trains its successors for purposes of the capitalist comeback", and that the right-leaning intellectuals "invariably try to make use of their influence surviving from the past to shape public opinion in preparation for the political and economic restoration of capitalism".

About five thousand posters — posters and slogans being an accepted way of making one's opinion known to the public in China — appeared in Peking. They attacked the policies pursued by the so-called scholar tyrants — meaning all those who insisted on the exaggerated reverence for scholars and intellectuals, and on the traditional "scholarly" style of teaching and examinations. There were too many subjects on the syllabus, and there were too many books. Altogether there was too much studying. Courses were too long, too formal, and too theoretical: from book to book, and from concept to concept, instead of being linked to practice — particularly to production. Students were being forced to submit themselves to the authority of the teacher and to learn by rote instead of being encouraged to develop originality and creativity. Examinations were conducted in too rigid a manner and tested memory instead of proficiency under practical conditions. Under the existing system, the children of the educated had a definite advantage over the children of the workers and peasants. As a result, the system created a new privileged class divorced from the masses instead of producing intellectuals from among the people, trained to serve and keep in touch.

On the ground that the schooling system needed an overhaul, all universities and secondary institutions were closed down. Red Defence Guards, a newly formed militant organization comprising mostly students and school-children released from their studies, emerged to "open fire against the anti-party anti-socialist black line". Their slogan was "Defend Mao Tse-tung" — implying that Chairman Mao was being threatened by conspiratorial forces that were plotting to deprive him of all power.

At first the Red Guards were hard pressed by counter-attacks led by those who had been doing much of the running of the country since the failure of the Great Leap Forward. This must have been what Mao had been planning for; for a few months he had disappeared from public view and in this way lulled the rightists into exposing themselves to attack. In August 1966 Mao put up his own big-character poster "Bombard the Headquarters" — meaning attack Liu Shao-chi and his associates within the party and the government. At a mass rally of the Red Guards held in Peking, about one million young people were inspected by Mao and Lin Piao, who placed their red bands on their own arms and handed them the right to "make revolt" against all those who wanted to restore the past. The Red Guards were declared to be the vanguard of the Cultural Revolution.

Once this was known, debate and rebellion spread all over the country. Red Guards, carrying and raising aloft a copy of the "little red book", roamed from place to place. In the name of the universal proletarian truth, with youthful fanaticism and exuberance, they attacked everything that seemed to them old, feudal, bourgeois, foreign, corrupt, or in any other way "counter-revolutionary". There was a wanton destruction of elements in China's literary and artistic heritage: statues were smashed, books were burned, and pictures were defaced. But their main target was people.

According to the rule book, the Red Guards were directed not so much against individuals as against their ideas and the state of their minds as revealed by their conduct. In order to "cure the illness and to save the patient", the emphasis was not on the use of force but on the use of reason, criticism, and debate. Rightists were to be given a way out so that they could turn over a new leaf. To give direction to the forces that had been unleashed, behind the Red Guards stood Chiang Ching, Mao's wife, and Lin Piao, who directed the army to back them up when necessary and to restrain them when they were getting out of hand.

By 1967 the struggle had been taken into the factories and all levels of party and government. Irrespective of whether a person was a party member, bureaucrat, manager, professor, writer, or artist, he could be subjected to criticism and molestation and even marched through the streets "crowned" with a tall paper hat on which slogans and accusations were written — an old Chinese custom of humiliating people. Gradually a trend towards hooliganism and near-anarchy developed. Thousands of "enemies of the people" were savagely beaten — many to the point of "suicide". There were also clashes between the Red Guards and other groups, and — because some factions were more extreme than others — among the Red Guards themselves. These clashes became increasingly violent and in some places reached such intensity that they destroyed public order. In large areas of the country, state administration broke down. The troubles in a number of major industrial centres and the transport problems created by the Cultural Revolution hampered output. Chou En-lai, the Chinese premier, admitted: "Economically speaking, China has had to pay dearly for so powerful a revolutionary movement." And China had to pay dearly not only economically; it has been reported that thousands of people died.

The course of events had turned out quite different from what Mao originally intended or expected. He never intended to stir up a turmoil of this magnitude; he merely wanted to remove from power a number of men who ran the country's superstructure and then allow the country to settle down again.

By the end of 1967, the most turbulent period was over. Schools had reopened, posters had been cleared from the hoardings, and the usual processions of drums had ceased. In 1968 the Red Guards were disbanded and dispersed back to their homes and into the countryside. Discipline was restored. But by this time the whole system had been shaken from top to bottom. A large number of prominent people had lost their positions. Among them were Liu Shao-chi, who was reviled as the "number one person in authority taking the capitalist road", the secretary of the party, the chief-of-staff of the army, the mayor of Peking, and the principal of the Peking University. Thousands more were forced to resign in disgrace. Many were sent to reform-through-labour farms to learn from the workers and peasants how to "integrate themselves with the masses".

The education system was thoroughly remodelled. Courses in general were shortened and simplified, and — because education had to teach the "correct" outlook — Mao Tse-tung Thought ranked high in education. The previous competitive examination method of enrolling students into institutions of higher education was abolished. Instead, before they could enter universities, young people were required to do manual labour in a commune for two years and then be "selected and recommended" by committees of peasants or workers on the strength of their moral, intellectual, and physical qualities. All academic titles were abolished so that lecturers should divest themselves of the attitudes of scholar-bureaucrats and to make teaching a reciprocal process requiring the active participation of the students as well as the teachers. Examinations were designed to test practical application rather than book learning and memory.

There was another aftermath to the Cultural Revolution. Because of the purges that had taken place, the party and bureaucratic cadres were in such disarray that the army had to take over the responsibility of administering the country. Lin Piao found himself in the forefront of political life and occupying a position of power in all fields of activity. In 1969 he was named Mao's "closest comrade in arms" and designated as his successor. But it seems that Mao — who had disliked his methods during the Cultural Revolution — was suspicious of his motives, and that Lin Piao thought that the only way he could ensure his succession was by neutralizing and, if necessary, by eliminating Mao. In 1971 he died in an aircraft crash in Outer Mongolia while attempting to escape to Russia. A few months later he was officially denounced as a traitor, conspirator, and would-be assassin of Mao.

In the years that followed, two alliances emerged within the Chinese leadership: one of the "radicals" and the other of the "moderates". The radicals placed a greater emphasis on continuing revolution and ideological purification, while the moderates emphasized production and material welfare. The radicals, who were associated with the egalitarian and mass mobilization programmes of the Cultural Revolution, received their support mainly from officials of all levels who had risen to prominence during the Cultural Revolution. They were incensed by the gradual rehabilitation of many of those removed from office in disgrace during the Cultural Revolution who were endangering their positions. The moderates, on the other hand, were prepared to see the patterns of power and the policies produced by the Cultural Revolution abandoned, and were willing to accept a degree of social and economic inequality for the sake of efficiency and economic modernization. They also wished to subordinate mass organizations to party discipline in order to lessen political convulsions. The role of Mao Tse-tung in this confrontation is not clear, although it would seem that he identified more with the radicals than with the moderates.

The radicals, who had acquired a strong influence over the central news media, made full use of them in their attempt to mobilize mass support for their programmes and for initiating "revolutionary great debates". During 1973-74 there was a campaign ostensibly directed against Lin Piao and Confucius.

The two were coupled because they were said to represent the ancient and the modern forces of reaction in China. The campaign died down after it failed to gather wide support, and Mao wrote: "The Cultural Revolution has been going on for eight years. It is now time for things to settle down." In 1975 there was another campaign which was directed towards the study of the theory of the dictatorship of the proletariat. It was followed by a campaign against the "rightist reversal of the correct verdict of the Great Proletarian Cultural Revolution" and all those who try to impede the progress of history. It came to an end in September 1976, when Mao died.

Hua Kuo-feng — who had occupied a middle-of-the-road position between the radicals and the moderates — became the new chairman of the Chinese Communist Party. He had the tacit support of the military and based his claim to leadership on a note supposed to have been written by Mao, which said: "With you in office, I can rest assured." He ordered the arrest of the leaders of the radical movement. The so-called Gang of Four included Mao's widow. Subsequently Teng Hsiao-ping was appointed vice-chairman of the party and vice-premier. Teng, a veteran of the Long March, was — before the Cultural Revolution — a member of the inner political bureau and the general secretary of the party. Because Mao had complained that, since 1959, Teng had not consulted him on anything, he was purged during the Cultural Revolution and paraded by the Red Guards through the streets wearing a dunce hat. He was later rehabilitated, only to be purged by Mao once again.

Hua and Teng appear to have taken up complimentary roles in order to bridge the gap between ideology and pragmatism. This kind of arrangement is something that seems quite acceptable to the Chinese "dialectic" mentality. There had been a somewhat similar relationship between Mao and Chou En-lai. The coalition that has assumed power is striving to prevent the recurrence of the civil strife, anarchy, and technological stagnation experienced during the "lost decade" (1966-76) — that is, during the Cultural Revolution and the years following it. Being dedicated to the "four modernizations" — agriculture, industry, national defence, and science and technology — they are trying to replace a revolutionary ideology with the unexciting but efficient rationality of modern society in order to make China a strong and prosperous country which should be at the very front rank of nations by the end of the century.

To achieve this goal, dramatic departures in administrative, economic, and educational policies are being initiated. In order to have greater central control, there are moves to make the party more disciplined and competent and to reinvest it with the authority that it enjoyed before the Cultural Revolution. There are changes in the management structure: "revolution-ary committees" are being replaced by a system of individual responsibility. Material incentives — various forms of bonuses and other schemes that peg incomes directly to output — are increasingly being authorized. Peasants are promised better prices for their produce and at the same time are exhorted to increase their contribution to what is called "basic capital for-mation" — that is, off-season work to reclaim wasteland, con-struct irrigation projects, level fields, terrace hillsides, and so forth. Foreign trade and tourism are promoted to earn foreign exchange so that China might be in a better position to import science and technology developed abroad.

The changes taking place in the area of education are drasti-cally curtailing or completely eliminating the most important reforms introduced during the Cultural Revolution. Examin-ations for admission to higher education have not only been reintroduced but have become rigorous and uniform, academic ranks and titles for lecturers have been reinstated, and teaching staff in general are being given greater authority over their classes. Moreover, high-quality schools for gifted youths are openly sanctioned and have the best teachers and facilities.

Because some of the reforms that are being introduced to launch the "New Long March" strike directly at the core values of the Chinese revolution — equality and national (economic) independence — there can be little doubt that this process of accelerated economic development and modern-ization will, at least in the short run, transform the substance of present society. The differences between town and country, between industry and agriculture, and between mental and manual labour may well be increasing instead of disappearing. The greater authority vested in the party and government administrative apparatuses will tend to widen the gap between the leaders and the masses. As a result of the priority given to rapid industrialization, one can expect that there will be a rising disparity between the urban and rural standards of living. Management by individuals instead of committees and more material incentives and fringe benefits will bring back the risk of élitism. The changes in the educational field may create a class of privileged people. Any schooling system in which admissions, promotions, and graduations are based on merit inherently favours urban over rural youth and those who have educated parents over those who have not.

Whether the modernization programme will succeed or not will depend largely on whether the present coalition remains united, despite the difficulties and associated tensions that modernization will inevitably create, and provide stable authority. China's central leadership must gain the kind of credibility that will encourage bureaucratic cadres at all levels to be fully committed to the new policy. Past experience has taught them that no policy line is permanent, regardless of how much it is being pushed by rhetoric, and that those who seized the initiative in implementing a controversial policy in the past often suffered badly when policy was reversed. This is, in fact, what has happened to the seventeen million young people who joined the party during the Cultural Revolution.

Apart from the possible leadership problems, the modernization programme may also be threatened by the widespread popular dissatisfaction it might generate. A fast pace of industrialization invariably means that fewer consumer goods are being produced and, as a result, the awakened expectations of the Chinese peasants and workers will not be met in the near future. Another source of popular discontent is the millions of urban youths who responded to the call to settle in the countryside when they finished their secondary schooling. They will now find that they lack the academic skills to pass tough examinations into universities and, consequently, will not have an opportunity to take a leading role in a modernizing society.

But, whatever happens, Maoism — or to use its proper name Marxism-Leninism-Mao Tse-tung Thought — can be expected to survive as China's frame of reference and its official belief system. It is very likely that Mao will be "desanctified", but not demolished. His writings — like those of Marx and Lenin, and those of all other large systems of thought — are diverse enough to lend themselves to manipulation in a way that will justify and legitimize ideologically any decision arrived at pragmatically by whoever is the leader and his immediate entourage.

The Chinese Communists — with sweat and tears but with as little blood as possible — have created a China that evokes a great deal of admiration and respect. They have made China a fiercely independent world power. Despite reverses, the average Chinese is certainly better off than he was before 1949, when he was ruled by virtually independent provincial military governors. He has free education, free medical services, compensation and old-age pension, and other forms of security. Streets are cleaner, and the beggars and prostitutes have disappeared. There are no black markets, corrupt officials, or organized crime and only a low rate of inflation. Probably no other country is more egalitarian than China is at present. Against this, the average Chinese lives a generally austere and regimented life. He has little choice of jobs; he can be deployed from factory to factory, from one type of work to another, and from locality to locality. And, China being an ideologically totalitarian party-state, he must follow the official line in his everyday life and action. The party's influence reaches into such personal matters as child rearing, sex habits, clothing styles, and manners — generally imposing a stern puritanical morality. If an individual lacks "social consciousness" or fails to display his belief in the political orthodoxy, he is subject to harassment that will embitter his life.

The Sino-Soviet Dispute

In the past the Chinese regarded themselves as the only real source of human civilization — and, as pointed out earlier, up to the nineteenth century they had good reason for doing so.

But since 1840 China had been subjected to humiliating foreign domination, to political and intellectual turmoil, and to forty years of civil and international wars. In 1949 Mao Tse-tung showed his resolve to defend China's national honour by declaring that it would "never again be an insulted nation".

While Stalin was alive, China accepted him as the ideological leader of the socialist camp. Being the leader of the "fatherland of socialism", Stalin was proclaimed the official interpreter of the "universal truth of Marxism-Leninism". This was despite the fact that, at times, Stalin had interfered with the Chinese revolution in order to subordinate its interests to those of the Soviet Union. After the Japanese surrender, he even tried to prevent the resumption of the civil war and displayed a distinct lack of enthusiasm for Mao, whom — like Tito of Yugoslavia — he might not be able to control once the country was under his rule.

Within a year of coming to power, Mao went to Moscow, where he spent two months. During his stay he concluded a trade agreement and signed a thirty-year Sino-Soviet Pact of Friendship and Alliance that could be invoked in the event of Japan or its allies — meaning the United States — attacking China. In the years that followed, the Chinese leadership — which had no experience in either socialist or economic construction — went along with the ideological and political line laid down by Moscow and copied the Soviet economic model.

By 1957 the Communists had established their complete control throughout the whole of China. This huge country was finally united and free of all strife. As it felt stronger, Chinese nationalism and self-esteem reasserted itself, and — now that Stalin was dead — the Chinese leadership assumed greater independence. In fact, Stalin's successors in the Soviet Union showed great deference to their Chinese counterparts, and Mao began exerting a claim to the ideological leadership of the international Communist movement. The new leader of this venerable nation set out to regain its dignity. From this background sprouted the Sino-Soviet rift.

The first outward sign of a split came in 1959 — only ten years after the declaration of "eternal and indestructible friendship". The Soviet Union suddenly abrogated the nuclear-

124 / Marxism as Political Ideology

sharing agreement, made only two years earlier, which had guaranteed protection to China. It did so because the Chinese leadership refused demands that Soviet troops virtually occupy the nuclear installations in China and that the two countries set up a joint fleet along China's coast. Behind all this was Mao's resolve that the new China — having acquired experience and expertise — now had to turn into a self-reliant nation, not only militarily but also economically. There was no longer any need to accept dogmatically the Soviet model of socialist construction. Soviet methods and other foreign methods would be analysed critically: what was bad in them would be rejected, and what was good would be accepted but applied "creatively" — meaning that a Chinese content would be added to it.

This new approach was fully reflected in the Great Leap Forward. As described earlier, the Chinese embarked upon a policy of fostering local initiative, small-scale industry, and revolutionary zeal; instead of following the Soviet practice of centralized planning, of giving high priority to heavy industry, and of sanctioning material incentives. In 1960, after the Chinese had ignored Soviet criticism of the communes and the policies pursued during the Great Leap Forward in general, all Soviet experts in China were recalled within one month and all technical assistance programmes terminated. The Russians even took back plans and blueprints essential for the completion of new plants and other projects. This aggravated the economic crisis China was passing through at the time.

In 1963 the publication by Peking of hostile letters exchanged between the Central Committee of the Chinese Communist Party and that of the Communist Party of the Soviet Union brought into the open the ideological and political differences underlying the dispute, a dispute that has been conducted in the tortuous and spiteful manner that has characterized intellectual disputes among Marxists whenever theory had to be adapted to political and economic developments in particular countries.

According to the Chinese, it all started in 1956 when, without prior consultation with fraternal parties, Khrushchev bitterly denounced Stalin. The Chinese Communists, who must have been afraid that the challenge to Stalin might endanger their own rule in China, conceded that Stalin had made some serious mistakes but stressed that nevertheless he had "creatively applied and developed Marxism-Leninism". His merits were more important than his mistakes. Because Stalin's actions merely reflected contradiction "between the individual and the collective in socialist society", Mao Tsetung in his discussions with Soviet leaders "waged a struggle against them in order to help them correct their errors". His fraternal urgings to "remould their thinking" and to revere Stalin's "correct side" must have annoyed the Soviet leaders, who chose not to follow his advice.

But there were wider grounds for the ideological dispute. After 1927, when the urban worker-centred bases of the Communist Party in China were destroyed, Mao evolved a grand new concept on how to contrive an armed revolt from rural base areas in the pre-industrialized regions of the world, instead of uprisings by the industrial proletariat in the big cities in advanced economies. This concept is said to be his most important contribution to Marxist-Leninist theory. He stressed the uniqueness of the Chinese revolution and how its experience could be applied to other underdeveloped countries where the basic political and economic conditions had many similarities to those in China during the civil war. He showed how to indoctrinate a discontented peasantry, and how to organize them to make and sustain a "people's war" — meaning a protracted guerilla war of liberation from feudalism and imperialism.

In the early 1960s, Mao decided that it was China's duty to "take up the heaviest burden" — that is, to become the leader of the world revolt. He had arrived at the conclusion that the Soviet Union had abdicated from its international revolutionary duty and escaped into "selfish, greedy, self-centred national interest". Thus the Chinese vision of China as the "central country" was openly revived. In 1965 Lin Piao published an article "Long Live the Victory of People's War", in which he expanded Mao's revolutionary concept to a new theory of global revolution. He stressed the point that the Chinese revolution served as a model not only for national liberation struggles but also for an all-embracing revolutionary strategy against imperialism. In China (unlike in Russia) the revolution started in the countryside and triumphed only towards the end in the cities. A similar pattern had to apply to world revolution. He defined Asia, Africa, and South America as the "rural areas of the world", and North America and Europe as the "cities of the world". In the "contemporary world revolutionary stage" this made Asia, Africa, and South America the centre of world revolution — that is, the "oppressed nations and people of Asia, Africa, and South America" were faced with the "urgent task of fighting imperialism and its lackeys" by carrying out their own revolutions and thus encircling North America and Europe. Only national democratic revolutions fought by the masses (comprising the workers, the peasants, the national bourgeoisie, and the revolutionary intellectuals) against feudalism and imperialism in these countries — followed by socialist revolutions — could resolve the "fundamental contradiction between states under the dictatorship of the proletariat and those under the dictatorship of the monopoly capitalist". But, in accord with Marxist-Leninist orthodoxy, although the peasantry represented the principal revolutionary force in these agrarian countries, this force had to be subordinated to the leadership of the proletariat.

While China was going to be "the staunch, reliable Red base" of the world revolutionary movement, it was repeatedly stressed that revolution could not be exported or imported. Revolutionary consciousness had to be aroused in each country separately, and in each country the revolution had to be fought by the people themselves in accordance with the prevailing conditions. The role of the socialist countries was not armed aggression but to provide arms, supplies, and moral support, in order to shorten the period of struggle and to reduce their losses.

The Soviet reaction was that the "concept of revolution as the struggle of the world village against the world city is tantamount to the rejection of the leading role of the working class and constituted a complete revision of the Marxist-Leninist doctrine of the historical mission of the working class". The Soviet leadership accused the Chinese of being dogmatists, adventurists, militant great-power chauvinists, and even of being madmen seeking war. It is obvious that the Soviet Union had no desire to be dragged into a nuclear conflict with the United States over issues not directly related to its interests. Khrushchev argued that the relationships among the forces of the world were constantly changing in favour of socialism, and consequently there was no necessity to promote dangerous wars of liberation in underdeveloped countries in an attempt to accelerate the process. The revolution need not take the form of force and mass action; there were peaceful forms of struggle that would bring the working class to power. Once socialist countries had established their economic and cultural superiority, socialism would spread by contagion.

The Chinese denounced this as "modern revisionism" — *modern* so as to contrast it with the revisionism in the German Social Democratic Party at the end of the nineteenth century. They argued that if the international Communist movement were one-sidedly reduced to "peaceful coexistence", "peaceful competition", and "peaceful transition", it would discard its historical mission of promoting world revolution. This would not only betray the revolutionary teachings of Marx and Lenin but would also erode the militancy of the revolutionaries throughout the world. They declared that modern revisionism represented the main danger being faced by the international Communist movement.

According to the Chinese, nuclear war was neither so likely nor its consequences, if it came, so unacceptable as to justify hesitancy in adopting a more militant international policy. Mao stated: "The atom bomb, which the American reactionaries use to frighten people with, is a paper tiger. It looks terrifying, but in reality it is not. It is, of course, a weapon that can cause vast massacres, but it is people who determine the result of a war, and not one or two new weapons." In other words, because in the long run men are stronger than weapons — however genocidal — a politically conscious people led by a dedicated revolutionary party would win in the end. Under constant and protracted harassment, at various points around the globe, the imperialists would be overextended and would disintegrate. Because "the people and the people alone" were the "motive force of world history", in the end power always belonged to them.

During the 1950s and early 1960s the Chinese Communists singled out the United States as the most viciously reactionary of all imperialist powers and, therefore, as the number one enemy of the peoples of the world. The United States was described as a country in which the injustices of capitalism were matched by the hypocrisies of its so-called democracy. And, as demonstrated by its support for Taiwan and its involvement in Vietnam, the United States was governed by warmongers seeking to control all the non-Communist world in order to consolidate its imperialist domination. The easing of the strained relations between the Soviet Union and the United States greatly contributed to the Sino-Soviet rift. In their antagonism, the Chinese went so far as to speak of a plot by the Soviet Union and the United States to encircle China with a ring of hostile countries and to rule the world.

The Soviet Union was not only accused of abandoning the international struggle and of even entering into collusion with the American imperialists, but also of its party and state leadership being "usurped by revisionists". In other words, the Soviet Union was taking the capitalist road instead of building a new society. While it had abolished private property, it had continued with the capitalist-style superstructure. The role and functions of the capitalists were taken over by a privileged stratum of the state burreaucracy. The Soviet Union was not becoming a truly classless society. The power, privileges, and access to education of the bureaucracy were setting up a new class separated from the rest of the people. The existence of material incentives and some free-market transactions, with their implications of selfish motivation, were further proof that the Soviet Union was abandoning the mental and spiritual aspects of the revolution and was heading towards the full restoration of the "bourgeois dictatorship".

Towards the end of the 1960s the Chinese stressed less and less the dangers of capitalist imperialism and more and more the dangers represented by revisionism, social imperialism, and Soviet hegemony. The Chinese leadership abandoned the view that the world was divided into blocs, and that China was a member of a socialist camp. Thus the ideological solidarity between the two "fraternal" parties came to an end. Even the state-to-state relations between China and the Soviet Union have cooled down to a freeze. As regards trade, Mao Tse-tung stated that there could not be much trade because Soviet products were heavy, crude, and high-priced and that the Russians always kept something back. It was better to deal with the bourgeoisie "who still have some business ethics".

4

A Review of Marx's Assumptions and Predictions

Marx's conception of history is built on the assumption that because of the constant necessity of having to provide for their material needs in order to survive, men are shaping history in conformity with certain "scientific" laws. According to these laws there is a tendency towards a sequence of epochs — moving from lower to higher forms of organization — which establish relations of production, exchange, and property that correspond to the character of the productive forces prevailing during the period. This concept allowed Marx to predict the dissolution of the capitalist system: by creating an increasingly numerous and impoverished working class, capitalism produced the very forces that would one day destroy it and create a communist society.

This historical model being the framework upon which Marx based his "scientific" theory, the most fundamental criticism is that no such pattern can be proved. History cannot be presented as a science because it is so full of happenings, many of them illogical, that it seems impossible to try to categorize them in a systematic fashion. Any generalization about the basic causes of social change in the historical movement of the human race is impossible. Nobody knows all the historical facts in all periods — and even if one person knew them, he could only evaluate them subjectively and in line with the current way of thinking. He would treat past events as though they were present happenings at some different time. In sum, critics say that historical reality is not quite as simple as Marx's theory would suggest, and one cannot predict how history will proceed and how it will end.

But even Marx, while emphasizing his laws of the evolution of history, wrote that history was "nothing but the activity of man pursuing his aims". Whether or not a historical pattern evolves and the speed at which it would evolve largely depend on whether the social classes — whose interests coincide with the developing tendencies — can raise the consciousness so as to change themselves and be in a position to take advantage whenever the opportunity offers itself to initiate and perpetuate a new social order. He also wrote about the relevance of "accidents" such as the character of those who stand at the head of the historically determining classes.

Although the thesis that history operates in accordance with an evolutionary pattern is today fully believed only by Marxists, Marx's theory of the great importance of economic factors in social change commands world-wide attention. It is accepted that the synthesis of contradictions within society is the motive force for many of the social changes, and that these changes are most pronounced whenever new material conditions of life emerge. At the time Marx wrote, economic factors were considered to be of no or little consequence in the course history was taking, and he brought about the realization that they must be important in a world in which the vast majority of the people were living in poverty and as a result were deprived of opportunities to develop their potentials.

Nevertheless, Marx is criticized on the grounds that he oversimplified the complexity of society. To argue that economic forces predominantly shape the fate of man ignores the realities of human nature. Material factors can be fundamental only as long as people lack an adequate amount of food, clothing, and shelter. Once their basic physiological needs are reasonably provided for, economics ceases to be the prime concern. More complex psychological needs — such as for safety, belonging, and self-respect — gain prominence, and, to have a satisfactory model of social structure, we must recognize that they shape many of society's values, ideas, and institutions. In fact there are times when the whole economic system tends to come under a cloud of distrust. If Marx were alive today, most probably he would not argue with the above reasoning. In 1893 Engels defined materialism. He wrote that materialism does not mean "that the economic situation is the cause, or is alone active while everything else is passive. Rather there is an interaction on the basis of economic necessity which in the last analysis always prevails." And he confessed: "Marx and I are partly to blame for the fact that younger writers sometimes lay more stress on the economic side than is due to it. We had to emphasize this main principle in opposition to our adversaries, who denied it, and had not always the time, the place or opportunity to allow the other elements involved in the interaction to come into their rights."

The assumption that is believed to be the foundation upon which Marx's whole conception was built is his theory about the relationship between human nature, freedom, and alienation. Marx held that man has an inner drive to realize a wide range of creative potentials, or powers, in order to develop himself into a "whole" human being; and, if he is denied the freedom to fulfil his potentials — that is, if he is alienated from what is rightfully his — it causes him psychological deprivation that moves him to revolutionary activity. Marx postulated that when man left the "realm of necessity" and entered the "realm of freedom", in which he could grow into what was in him to become, he would join in genuine and harmonious co-operation with all others.

Critics say that psychological deprivation is more likely to lead to political apathy than to revolutionary activity. Besides, not everybody experiences it. Moreover, it is very doubtful that a communist society would do away with it because, only too often, psychological deprivation has its source in individual characteristics, neurotic tendencies, and frustrations in a person's private life.

But no real test on Marx's theory is possible until the society envisaged by him comes into being and man is free both to engage in any activity he chooses and to interact with all of his fellow men. Only then will one be able to establish whether man has an urge to satisfy a variety of latent abilities, whether he has it in him to co-operate rationally with others, and indeed whether there can be a society in which the complete fulfilment of each individual is compatible with that of all others.

It is argued that Marx's proposition that labour is the source of all value often causes Marxist economies to use both labour and non-labour resources irrationally and inefficiently. Some of these resources can be very scarce and non-renewable. In market economies their high prices would ensure that they are sparingly used. Also, because of Marx's concept of surplus value, interest on the investment capital employed tends to be disregarded as a legitimate cost and, as a consequence, the real cost of the investment might not be properly estimated. For instance, in the Soviet Union many resources were tied down for a very long time in the construction of a huge hydro-electric station. Had interest on the cost of the resources used in the capital investment been calculated it would have become obvious that thermal-power plants — which can be constructed more quickly and put to use earlier — would have brought about a better allocation of resources.

Moreover, Marx's idea of central planning as an integral part of the socialist society is said to cause Marxian economies to bog down. Where there is planning there is always the risk of misplanning. The more ambitious a plan is, the greater the risk. Also, planning can introduce rigidity into the complex economic process of an industrial society and thus lead to a general inability to adapt to changing conditions and local circumstances. Above all else, it is not necessarily true that the bureaucrats at the central planning points are better judges of what is good for the people than the people themselves. In free-enterprise economies a market mechanism indicates — though not in a perfect fashion — the relative consumer preferences for the thousands of goods and services produced in the country.

Now what about Marx's predictions? History has never been kind to its prophets: the world is unlike the world anyone has predicted. Marx too has proved to have been a poor prophet. The forecasts he made a century ago have been mocked by what has happened since. Those that may still come true are unlikely to come about in the manner he expected.

Marx's dictum that man cannot progress politically, socially, and economically until the capitalist social order has been

destroyed has been disproved by subsequent events. He grossly underestimated the vitality and adaptability of the free-
enterprise society. It did change. Forces have arisen — no
doubt accelerated by the challenges posed by Socialist parties
and other groups influenced by the Marxian philosophy — that
made for a wider sharing of the ever-increasing wealth and for
the development of the modern welfare state. In sum, there
are less drastic solutions to the ills of capitalism than a revolutionary expropriation of the expropriators.

In the industrialized societies the state has not become the
tool of the ruling classes dominated by the industrial capitalists. State political power is shared with politicians, top public
servants, the "labour aristocracy" in the trade unions, professional people, and others. Moreover, as a rule, those who
wield power must act in sympathy with public opinion. "Capitalist" countries are gradually developing into what are rightly
described as socialized societies without recourse to a dictatorship of the proletariat. The state itself is involved in the
economic process; it encourages a degree of national economic
planning and circumscribes the activities of producers and dis-
tributors. There is a broad legislative framework relating to
company organization, restrictive practices, private property,
and so on. It levies high taxes on companies and big private
incomes; and a high proportion of government receipts is used
to promote general education, health, and social services.

Marx believed quite incorrectly that the working class
would have no real political power in capitalist societies.
Already towards the end of the nineteenth century workers
had received full franchise in most industrialized countries.
They formed their own political parties and elected their
leaders to become members of parliament. In fact, the
workers' political influence had advanced to such a degree that
in the 1880s Engels was to write: "And so it came about that
the bourgeoisie and government feared more the legal than
the illegal actions of the workers' party, more the successes of
the election than those of rebellion."

Society has not polarized into a small group of extraordi-
narily wealthy capitalists facing an anormous mass of improv-
erished workers. The political organization of labour and the

acceptance of trade unions as part of the social order have led
to state intervention in industrial matters and to collective bargaining. Child labour has been abolished, and the hours of
work and working conditions in general have improved
greatly. There is no huge reserve army of the unemployed to
grind down the conditions of the employed workers. Even the
farmers, whom Marx dismissed as being without a class consciousness and therefore without an organization, have since
organized themselves and forced protectionist policies in virtually every major Western country.

All this has made nonsense of Marx's notion of an ever-
increasing misery among the masses. While it is true that the
rich have grown richer, it is not true that the workers have
grown poorer. They too have become better off. The proportions of profits and wages in the gross domestic product
figures of the industrial countries remained, to a surprising
degree, constant for the hundred years preceding the Second
World War. Since then the share of wages has tended to rise.
Already during Marx's lifetime the standard of living of the
working class had improved. Marx countered that under capitalism the workers were always exploited because they could
buy back less with the wages received than they had produced
earning those wages. Moreover, even if the standard of living
of the workers temporarily rose, their exploitation would intensify if they could acquire proportionally less of their own
product than before. Marx also recognized psychological im-
poverishment. He wrote that a "house may be large or small,
as long as the surrounding houses are equally small it satisfies
all social demands for a dwelling. But let a palace arise beside
the little house, and it shrinks from a little house to a hut" and
its occupants "feel more and more uncomfortable, dissatisfied
and cramped within its four walls".

The wealthy bear only remote resemblance to Marx's idea
of the capitalist. They are not the sole owners of all the factors
of production and distribution. The rapid extension of joint
stock companies (in which shareholders have their liability
limited to the amount they actually invest in the company) has
created a situation in which companies are not collectively
owned only by a few capitalists, as Marx believed, but also by a

large number of "mini-capitalists" — that is, people who have acquired small share holdings. Thus the wealthy are sharing the ownership of the means of production with middle-class shareholders. This middle, or intermediate, class — instead of being squeezed out of existence as Marx predicted — has grown in number. Its members have neither become part of the proletariat nor tried to stop the development of capitalism and return to small-scale production methods. But, instead of being self-employed artisans, farmers, and shopkeepers, they are in the main a middle-income class of salaried employees.

And not only is it that the wealthy are denied sole ownership of the productive process; the effective control of it also is largely eluding them. Today the managerial — that is, the decision-making — positions in government and business organizations belong to the professional managers, who in increasing numbers come from the non-wealthy class. Because they exercise managerial power although they own no property, ownership and control of the means of production are being separated within the system.

The supplanting of the capitalists by managers was recognized by Marx himself, but only late in his life. In 1940 a book was published which attracted a great deal of attention. It was written by an ex-Communist, John Burnham, and called *The Managerial Revolution*. Burnham made an attempt to reconcile Marxian concepts with the realities of the time. He ascribed to the managerial class (as Lenin did to the "financiers") all the power and political influence attributed by Marx to the capitalist class. However ingenious, Burnham's argument cannot be sustained.

Today managers are not a class, only a kind of élite. So far they have made no concerted effort to acquire political power. Their organizations have progressed no fruther than being another pressure group within the community — alongside the trade unions, churches, farmers' organizations, and many others. Managers, as a rule, are self-effacing men who merely seek to produce enough profits to satisfy shareholders and thus retain their positions, prestige, and income without developing ulcers. They are subjected to various pressures. Apart from having their actions circumscribed by a wide range of government legislation, they are caught in a squeeze: on the one hand there is competition in the market, and on the other hand they are faced with well-organized trade unions demanding more pay and better working conditions.

Another of Marx's expectations, that the rate of profit — that is, return on investment — would decline, has been proved wrong. As a result, capital accumulation continued to grow instead of falling away. However, as time passed, the consolidation of production into huge aggregates did take place within the industrializing economies. Marx therefore was right in holding that capitalism tends towards a concentration of capital. "Big business" grew and acquired substantial control over markets, and a large number of small producers were eliminated. To curb this monopolizing tendency that threatened to destroy free competition — the idea on which the free-enterprise system was founded — anti-trust laws were passed in a number of countries by the end of the nineteenth century. Today monopolies still exist, but they have to temper blatant monopolistic practices with caution. They have come to realize that an adverse effect on public opinion may not only harm them in the market but also lead to additional restrictive legislation or even to the nationalization of the industry.

Marx's prophecy that remained true for a very long time was that economic crises are going to last longer and become more violent as time passes. The depression of the 1930s reached such proportions that even the most ardent opponents of Marx came to suspect that he may have been a realist after all. People in general came to accept the notion that there must be something very wrong with a system that allows such high levels of unemployment, dislocation, and misery.

Nonetheless, in the industrially advanced countries, the mood growing out of the 1930s depression acted as a catalyst for reforming the system instead of producing a proletarian revolution. Governments, searching for a solution, began to accept the new economic approach that was being advocated by Keynes and a number of other economists. They dispensed with the hitherto sacrosanct balanced budgets and by way of fiscal and other measures deliberately manipulated the demand for goods and services in such a manner as to maintain it at a level that would allow for virtually full employment. Since the Second World War — in the so-called post-Keynesian world — no advanced industrial country has experienced a real depression. There were only minor depressions, named recessions, that were caused mainly by measures designed to slow down an overstimulated and booming economy. However, Keynesian policies, by removing fear of depression created a level of confidence and expectations that resulted in Western societies being ravaged by inflation instead. This, in turn, brought about business uncertainty and an increase in the number of those unemployed.

No such thing as an international revolutionary working class-consciousness has developed. Marx predicted that the worker would abandon nationalistic allegiances and take up loyalties only to his class because the conflict between the propertied and the property-less class was the only fundamental and significant quarrel within society. As it turned out Marx had grossly underestimated the social importance of nationalism, and national sentiments and interests prevailed. The wage workers, instead of becoming a proletarian vanguard, have been incorporated into nationalist capitalism. In a number of wars, workers from one country were prepared to fight those from another. And in no advanced economy have workers readily accepted foreign labour which might have threatened the security of their jobs. Trade unions and labour parties function in a reformist manner within the system: they strive for a greater share of the national product rather than for progress towards a proletarian revolution. In fact, trade unions have a vested interest in the system because their survival depends on the freedom to organize being basic principle of the political order.

According to Marxist dialectics, all socialist revolutions would take place only where the proletariat had become conscious of its historic role and where it would inherit the achievements of a mature capitalist system. There would be in existence an abundance of the means of production and distribution, of skills and experience, and a superstructure that underpinned industrial production. This was a prerequisite for the revolution to establish a society in which, in due course, there would be goods and services for all according to their needs, freedom to develop each man's many-sided potentials, and spontaneous and genuine co-operation. But the revolutions that took place in Russia, China, Yugoslavia, and Cuba (communism imposed through external coercion, such as was the case in Eastern Europe and North Korea, have no relevance whatsoever to Marx's theory) were in countries where there was an all-round scarcity rather than an abundance. They caused the collapse of non-industrialized feudal systems in which the regimes had shown political disintegration. Industrialization followed the revolution instead of preceding it. Nor were the revolutions carried out in the true Marxian sense; they were not the actions of a disciplined, well-organized and class-conscious proletariat aware of its historic mission. They were engineered, in the name of the proletariat, by a relatively small number of people who relied on the support of the peasantry. They argued that in economically backward countries a small party can represent the proletariat as the revolutionary agent and do the work of industrialization and modernization that is being done by the capitalists in other countries.

In those countries which today regard themselves as Communist and acknowledge Marx as their ideological ancestor, the state shows no sign of withering away and the workers are nowhere in the process of capturing power that they could exercise through freely elected bodies. Instead, the "vanguards of the proletariat" have established themselves in what appears to be a permanent authority over the whole people. They exercise their power through the administrative bureaucracy and not only suppress all political opposition but also oppose every kind of ideological dissent. Although in theory the workers are now the owners of the means of production, in most Communist countries there is a total party-government monopoly over the economy and other basic spheres of life. The worker is at least as much under the control of the party-bureaucratic élite as workers in the non-Communist countries are under the control of their capitalist managers.

As already noted, Marx — like most of the other radical thinkers of his time — was passionate about individual freedom and growth and blamed the capitalist system for keeping the individual from coming to "self-consciousness of himself, of his position in society, and of his true interests". Marx predicted that when the communist society came into being, because man would have conquered his environment and all of the sustenance for human growth would be available to him, he would spontaneously co-operate with his fellow men. By common reasoning he would achieve a full, secure and dignified life. Reason and freedom of self-expression would flower side by side as they are part of man's real nature. This is one of those utopian dreams that remain to be tested — and it is very doubtful that it would survive the test in full. Man has an all-pervading need for safety, and he can feel safe only if the other members of his society are forced to conform to a defined set of rules as regards their behaviour. Conformity leads to familiarity and familiarity to security. Because of this basic psychological need, every society develops a culture designed to ensure an orderly and predictable existence. Despite lip-service to individuality, no society tolerates individualists. While some nonconformity is always accepted, clear limits are set and those who cross this borderline of tolerance are subjected to sanctions. These can vary from ridicule to ostracism. In more extreme cases nonconformists go to prison or mental asylum. Therefore, it is most unlikely that any future society will ever accept Marx's belief that there can be complete harmony between the individual and society, and that in each man freedom and reason automatically flower side by side. It is hard to imagine that man will ever abandon the type of social order that preserves "law and order" and live in what perhaps could be compared to a nation-wide artists' colony.

Now let us sum up. Marx's theory and his predictions have by and large been proved wrong. The state of the world does not fit into the Marxist analysis. Even if some of his predictions still come true, they will not come about in the way he expected them to. The main reason is that Marx was a nineteenth century figure. His ideas were conceived when conditions were very different from what they are today. He knew only the type of society he witnessed in Western Europe, and he projected from it into the past and the future.

But one must look beyond any logical, or factual, virtues and defects in Marx's conception. Judged on its broad intellectual and political impact, his work adds up to much more than a list of faulty assumptions and unfulfilled prophecies. Right or wrong, some of his ideas have earned great academic respect and occupy an important place in the European intellectual tradition, while his theory has been a major force in shaping the world we know today. Revolutionary movements were, and still are, well served by his work. It provides those dissatisfied with society with much needed theoretical ammunition.

Although a consistent theme underlies his whole work, one can distinguish between three Marxes. The first is the young Marx — the Young Hegelian — an ethical philosopher, a humanist and a moralist, concerned with alienation, or denial, of man's full development. The second is Marx the revolutionary of the late 1840s: an agitator with the hot gospel of the immediate overthrow of the existing social order. The third Marx is the mature Marx: an empirical sociologist who saw his task as giving a "scientific" base to socialism and, by doing so, bringing to the consciousness of the working class the nature of the act that is its destiny to accomplish.

Marxism, like other great ideologies, has disintegrated into diverse alignments in the course of time and as circumstances have changed. Marx's followers, by way of revision and elaboration, evolved a variety of "roads to socialism", each with its own doctrine and strategy. And each claims that it is Marx's legitimate heir because it is the closest to his real intentions. In other words, as there are three Marxes to choose from, and because there are some inconsistencies and unresolved questions in Marx's writings, the search for which is the "real" Marx is answered by which is the most applicable in the particular conditions. It is what may be called "selective identification"; and, to bridge the gap between Marx's conception and practice so that the two can exist side by side, there is a huge expenditure of intellectual resources.

The German Social Democrats were closest to the mature Marx and his scientific socialism. They established a mass party and aimed at educating the working class into developing a unity of purpose and a determination to vote themselves into power. The revolution was to be carried out through the polling-booths. This is still the most widely accepted type of socialism in those economically advanced countries in which there are constitutional means to capture state power without violence.

The Bolsheviks — or Marxist-Leninists — represented militant Marxism, which can be best related to Marx of the late 1840s. In the *Communist Manifesto* he wrote that the Communists were "the most advanced and resolute section of the working-class parties in every country, that section which pushes forward all others" as they had "the advantage of clearly understanding the line of march, the conditions, and the ultimate general results of the proletarian movement"; and when in 1848 the "middle class did not make its own revolution" Marx urged the working class to do it for them. The strategy of the Marxist-Leninists is based on a small determined body of revolutionaries, the "vanguards of the people", who speed up events instead of waiting for them to develop. They are prepared for the immediate conquest of power should the opportunity arise, and to industrialize the country themselves instead of standing at the sidelines until the capitalists do it. Theirs is the road propagated for the industrially backward countries. It has proved a speedy way to industrialize. With iron political control, they can hold down mass consumption to the subsistence level in order to accumulate capital.

Of late, in a number of Western countries, there has been a shift to the young Marx. In these countries, Marxist scholarship stresses Marx's early writings (discovered and published in the 1920s and of which early Marxists, including Lenin, had no knowledge), in which Marx clearly postulates the individuality and uniqueness of man. They show that Marx's fundamental commitment was to rescue man from the alienation he is fated to suffer in societies built on the division of labour and private property — more particularly in capitalist society. This new strain of "philosophical Marxism" has made important inroads on radical thinking and action. It became part of what was known as the New Left movement, and some of its aspects are incorporated into the policies formulated by the Eurocommunist parties.

The ideals and policies of the New Left movement, which was so prominent during the 1960s, are ambiguous because people joined for various reasons. It was a coalition of Marxists, anarchists, student radicals, women's liberationists, and quite liberal civil rightists, which came into its own in 1956 — the year of the violent suppression by Russian troops of the Hungarian revolt and the Soviet admission of Stalin's tyranny. The invasion of Czechoslovakia in 1968 (which put an end to the reforms that were introduced during the "Prague spring" to bring about "socialism with a human face") and the trials of dissidents in the Soviet Union reinforced the New Left. More and more leftists came to realize that the model of "socialist construction" developed in the Soviet Union was not the kind of life that would be acceptable in advanced countries with democratic traditions.

The Marxist elements in the New Left movement have their intellectual forerunners in the Hungarian Marxist George Lukacs and the Italian Marxist Antonio Gramsci, and their chief spokesmen in Herbert Marcuse — who was a member of the so-called Frankfurt School of social Marxists and, after Hitler came to power, moved to the United States — and the French existentialist Jean-Paul Sartre. They emphasized the will of the human subject — that is, the voluntary nature of revolutionary action. In other words, revolution is something that is decided by men and not predestined by a historical dialectic process as Marxism was being interpreted at the time of the Second International.

This new ideology is embraced primarily by the intellectual class — especially by students in the humanities — but not by the working class. These "university Marxists" maintain that Marx was right to become "materialist" and give a scientific base to socialism. At the time when Marx was developing his theory, material necessity stood in the way of achieving a lasting new and better system of human relations. But the capitalist system has since then created the material abundance that is the prerequisite for the free society Marx so passionately desired in which men co-operate naturally and — being the masters of their own destiny — develop into unalienated, or total, human beings. As the striving towards this kind of life

is the true spirit and substance of Marxism, Marx's non-philo-
sophical work should now be set aside and the proletariat and
the party should no longer be regarded as the main agents of
social change.

Select Bibliography

There are a great number of books, pamphlets, articles, and other material dealing with one aspect or another of this diverse and complex subject labelled Marxism. Below is only a brief guide to further reading. It is a list of books which, on the basis of subjective assessment, should be easily understood by the average reader. They were valuable props in the preparation of this book, and anyone seeking further knowledge would be well advised to choose one or more of them. Most are available in paperback editions and do not make heavy demand on the reader's pocket.

Bottomore, T.B., and Rubel, Maximilien, eds. *Karl Marx — Selected Writings in Sociology and Social Philosophy.* Harmondsworth, Mddx.: Penguin, 1963.

Brulé, Jean-Pierre. *China Comes of Age.* Harmondsworth, Mddx.: Penguin, 1971.

Carew-Hunt, R.N. *The Theory and Practice of Communism.* Harmondsworth, Mddx.: Penguin, 1963.

Chamberlin, William Henry. *The Russian Revolution.* New York: Universal Library, 1965.

Cole, G.D.H. *The Meaning of Marxism.* Ann Arbor: University of Michigan Press, 1964.

Deutscher, Isaak. *Trotsky — The Prophet Armed.* London: Oxford University Press, 1954.

_____ *Trotsky — The Prophet Unarmed.* London: Oxford University Press, 1959.

_____ *Stalin — A Political Biography.* Rev. ed. Harmondsworth, Mddx.: Penguin, 1966.

Fischer, Ernst. *Marx in His Own Words.* Harmondsworth, Mddx.: Penguin, 1973.

Fitzgerald, C.P. *Birth of Communism in China.* Harmondsworth, Mddx.: Penguin, 1964.

———. *The Chinese View of Their Place in the World.* London: Oxford University Press, 1967.

———. *Mao Tse-tung and China.* Harmondsworth, Mddx.: Penguin, 1977.

Freedman, Robert. ed. *Marx on Economics.* Harmondsworth, Mddx.: Penguin, 1962.

Getzler, Israel. *Martov.* Melbourne: Melbourne University Press, 1967.

Han Suyin. *China in the Year 2001.* Harmondsworth, Mddx.: Penguin, 1970.

Hudson, G.F. *Fifty Years of Communism — Theory and Practice 1917-1967.* Harmondsworth, Mddx.: Penguin, 1971.

Kamenka, Eugene. *The Ethical Foundation of Marxism.* 2nd ed. London: Routledge and Kegan Paul, 1972.

Kochan, Lionel. *The Making of Modern Russia.* Harmondsworth, Mddx.: Penguin, 1963.

Lukes, Steven. *Essays in Social Theory.* London: Macmillan, 1977.

MacIntyre, Alasdair. *Marxism and Christianity.* Harmondsworth, Mddx.: Penguin, 1971.

McLellan, David. *Marx before Marxism.* Rev. ed. Harmondsworth, Mddx.: Penguin, 1972.

———. *Marx's Grundrisse.* St Albans: Paladin, 1973.

———. *Karl Marx — His Life and Thought.* Frogmore: Paladin, 1976.

Marcuse, Herbert. *Soviet Marxism — A Critical Analysis.* Harmondsworth, Mddx.: Penguin, 1971.

Marx, Karl, and Engels, Friedrich. *The Communist Manifesto* (with an introduction by A.J.P. Taylor). Harmondsworth, Mddx.: Penguin, 1967.

Mills, C. Wright. *The Marxists.* Harmondsworth, Mddx.: Penguin, 1963.

Nicolaievsky, Boris, and Maenchen-Helfen, Otto. *Karl Marx — Man and Fighter.* Harmondsworth, Mddx.: Penguin, 1976.

Ollman, Bertell. *Alienation — Marx's Concept of Man in Capitalist Society.* Cambridge: Cambridge University Press, 1971.

Robinson, Joan. *An Essay in Marxian Economics.* London: Macmillan, 1947.

———. *The Cultural Revolution in China.* Harmondsworth, Mddx.: Penguin, 1970.

Schram, Stuart. *Mao Tse-tung.* Harmondsworth, Mddx.: Penguin, 1966.

_____. *The Political Thought of Mao Tse-tung.* Rev. ed. New York: Vintage Paperbacks, 1970.

_____. *Mao Tse-tung Unrehearsed.* Harmondsworth, Mddx.: Penguin, 1974.

Shub, David. *Lenin.* Rev. ed. Harmondsworth, Mddx.: Penguin, 1966.

Snow, Edgar. *Red Star over China.* Rev. ed. Harmondsworth, Mddx.: Penguin, 1972.

_____. *China's Long Revolution.* Harmondsworth, Mddx.: Penguin, 1974.

Smart, Ninian. *Mao.* Glasgow: Fontana/Collins, 1974.

Sweezy, Paul M. *Theory of Capitalist Development.* New York: Monthly Review Press, 1942.

Index

Central Committee of, 76, 86,
124; congress, 76, 79
communists, 8, 73, 84, 92, 142
competition, 17, 18, 30, 31, 33, 36,
37, 46, 68, 137; among workers,
40-41; free (market), 30, 67, 91,
137
*Conditions of the Working Class in
England*, 6
Confucius, 90, 118
consciousness, 20, 21; class, 29, 59,
135, 139; proletarian, 39, 40
Constitution of the Chinese People's
Republic (1954), 102
consumer goods, 44, 109, 121
consumption, 43; under-, 38
contradictions, 16, 22, 23, 100,
103-5, 131; antagonistic *and* non-
antagonistic, 104-5; objective *and*
subjective, 25
co-operatives, 51, 57, 81, 99
credit unions, 51
crime, 45
"crisis of Marxism", 60
Critique of the Gotha Programme, 55
Cuba, 139
Cultural Revolution, The Great
Proletarian, 113-21
Czechoslovakia, 88, 89, 143

Declaration of Independence of 1776
(American), 1
Declaration of the Rights of Man of
1789 (French), 1
democratic centralism, 77, 110
depression (economic), 138; of the
1930s, 94, 137. *See also* economic
crisis
détente, 89
Deutsch-Französische Jahrbücher, 5
dialectic, 15, 21, 22, 23, 63, 103, 104,
119, 143
dialectics, 15 (definition of), 138
dictatorship, 77, 79; bourgeois, 128;
of the monopoly capitalist, 126; of
the party, 77, 80; of the
proletariat, 42, 43, 53, 65, 70, 71,
77, 81, 82, 84, 85, 88, 89n, 103,

106, 112, 119, 126, 134; of the
proletariat and peasantry, 86; over
the proletariat, 65; over the
proletariat and peasantry, 86;
personal, 80
division of labour, 12, 18, 19, 20, 22,
23, 26, 27, 29, 34, 35, 46, 142
dogmatism, 95, 96

economic, 26, 38, 59, 87, 120, 131;
crisis(es), 9, 10, 11, 31, 38, 41, 50,
51, 137
*Economic and Philosophic Manuscript
of 1844*, 55
economics, 6, 21
"economism", 66
education, 25, 27, 44, 46, 53, 57, 58,
128, 134; in China, 93n, 98, 100,
101, 105, 107, 114, 117, 120-22; of
workers, 7, 51
*Eighteenth Brumaire of Louis
Bonaparte, The*, 55
élite *and* élitism, 112, 121, 139
Engels, Friedrich, 1, 5, 6, 7, 8, 12,
19, 21, 41, 52, 55, 62, 63, 131, 134
England, 10, 52, 53, 107. *See also*
Britain
equality, 53, 76, 81
Essence of Christianity, 16
Estonian insurrection, 79
Eurocommunism(ts), 88, 89, 89n,
142
Europe, 69, 78, 86, 90, 92, 126;
before First World War, 4, 6, 7, 9,
11, 50, 52, 56, 58, 59, 60; Eastern,
83-86, 139; Western, 28, 56, 65,
72, 78, 83, 85, 90, 140
European: intellectual tradition, 141;
liberalism, 85
evolutionary (historic) pattern *or*
process, 28, 39, 65, 131. *See also*
historical evolutionary process
exploit, 25, 26, 33, 47, 68, 73, 81, 114
exploitation, 6, 8, 12, 30, 31, 40, 74,
98, 110, 135; rate of, 32-33

Fabian Society, 58
fascism, 83; anti-, 81

Middle Ages, 24
mir, 61
"moderates", 118, 119
modernization, 120, 121
modes of production. *See* production
money, 30, 34n, 43, 45, 75, 76
monopolies, 37, 67, 68, 137
monopolization, 31
morality, 17, 26, 73
Moscow, 70, 73, 84, 85, 92, 123
mutual-aid: societies, 67; teams, 95, 99

Napoleon, 4
narodniks *or* populists, 61-63, 66
National Party Congress, 102
Neue Rheinische Zeitung, 9, 10, 55
"new democracy", 97, 102
New Economic Policy, 75, 80
New Left, 142-43
New Long March, 120
New York, 54
New York Daily Tribune, 11
North America, 126
North Korea, 139

On Contradictions, 104
"On the Correct Handling of
  Contradictions among the
  People", 104
*On the People's Democratic
  Dictatorship*, 97
Opium War, 90
"opportunism", 65, 66, 68

Paris, 5, 6, 7, 9, 10
Paris Commune of 1871, 51-53, 58
Peace Conference of Versailles, 91
"peace movements", 88
peasant(ry), 36, 59, 61-64, 70, 72
Peking (Beijing), 114, 115, 124;
  mayor of, 117, University of, 91,
  117
"people's democracy", 84
"people's democratic dictatorship",
  97, 98
People's Republic of China, 97
"people's war", 125

"permanent revolution", 11, 78;
  Chinese concept of, 104
Petrograd, 70. *See also* Saint
  Petersburg
philosophy, 3; German, 1, 5, 13, 14;
  Greek, 14, 15; of history, 14, 15,
  25; "true", 22
planning, 108, 109n, 133; authority,
  43; national economic, 87, 99,
  124, 134
Plekhanov, G.V., 61, 65
Poland, 88; revolt of 1863, 50
political: awareness, 40, 74; power,
  26, 42-43; 44, 76, 136
Political Bureau *or* Politburo: China,
  102, 119; Soviet Union, 76
populists. *See* narodniks
Potemkin (battleship), 66
Potresov, Alexander, 65
Poverty of Philosophy, 55
powers, human: natural, 17; species,
  17-18, 35
"Prague spring", 143
Pravda, 77
production, 18, 22, 27-28, 36, 37, 43,
  48, 86, 115, 118; anarchy of, 27;
  factors of, 135; forces of, 21,
  23-25, 34, 37, 40; instruments *or*
  tools, of, 34, 43; intellectual, 21;
  mass, 34, 36; material, 2, 21, 27;
  means of, 20, 23, 25-27, 29, 37,
  39, 44, 47, 56, 67, 86, 103, 109,
  109n, 136, 138, 139; modes of, 20,
  21, 24, 26, 27, 30, 37, 53, over-, 38;
  team, 109n
productive: activity, 18, 35; assets,
  17, 18, 32, 33; base, 20; capacity,
  29, 31, 38; force, 19-21, 24, 28, 39,
  41, 43, 47, 78, 130; methods *or*
  techniques, 18, 23, 25, 28, 31, 33,
  136; reality, 23, 25; relations, 19,
  20, 21, 23, 24, 39, 47, 130
productivity, 31, 33, 36, 38, 78
"product of labour", 32, 34
profits, 30, 31, 32, 37n, 38, 135, 136;
  rate of, 37, 37n, 38, 137; super, 68
proletarian: class-conscious purpose,
  40; democracy, 79, 85;